Here + Now Scottish Art 1990–2001

Scottish Art since 1945

HERE

Aberdeen Art Gallery
Dundee Contemporary Arts
Generator Projects
McManus Galleries
Peacock Visual Arts

+ NOW

Scottish Art 1990–2001

Here + Now · Scottish Art 1990–2001
published to coincide with the exhibition
15 September – 4 November 2001

Aberdeen Art Gallery
Schoolhill · Aberdeen AB10 1FQ
T: 01224 523700
F: 01224 632133
Aberdeen City Council

Dundee Contemporary Arts
152 Nethergate · Dundee DD1 4DY
T: 01382 606220
F: 01382 606221
www.dca.org.uk
Supported by the Scottish Arts Council and Dundee City Council

Generator Projects
25–26 Mid Wynd · Dundee DD1 4JG
T / F: 01382 225982
www.generatorprojects.com
Supported by Dundee City Council and the Scottish Arts Council

McManus Galleries
Albert Square · Dundee DD1 1DA
T: 01382 432084
F: 01382 432052
E: arts.heritage@dundeecity.gov.uk
Dundee City Council Arts & Heritage

Peacock Visual Arts
21 Castle Street · Aberdeen AB11 5BQ
T: 01224 639539
F: 01224 627094
www.peacockvisualarts.co.uk
Supported by the Scottish Arts Council and the Aberdeen City Council

Published by Dundee Contemporary Arts
ISBN 0 9535178 7 X
Essays © the authors and Dundee Contemporary Arts
Edited by Katrina M. Brown and Rob Tufnell
Designed by Dalrymple · Printed by BAS

**Here + Now is supported by The Scottish Arts Council
and sponsored by The Royal Bank of Scotland and Scotland on Sunday
Publication supported by The Hope Scott Trust**

⁂ The Royal Bank of Scotland

The Royal Bank of Scotland is proud to be the principal sponsor of *Here + Now: Scottish Art 1990–2001*. This exhibition reflects the innovation and vision of Scottish culture and enterprise today and we are delighted to be associated with it. The strong selection of internationally renowned and respected artists – being shown in galleries and museums (both traditional and contemporary) in two of the country's key cities (Dundee and Aberdeen) – combines qualities that complement the Royal Bank's own values as a leading UK and international bank, headquartered in Scotland.

The Royal Bank has a long tradition of supporting visual art and the sponsorship of exhibitions such as *Here + Now* is an important part of our programme.

It is, however, only a part of a bigger picture. For example, the Royal Bank of Scotland Art Awards, run in conjunction with the Friends of the Royal Scottish Academy, has been encouraging the practice of young artists for more than seven years. The Bank also maintains its own art collection which, since our acquisition of NatWest last year, is one of the UK's largest corporate collections with more than 3,500 works spanning some 300 years. Indeed, some of the artists in this exhibition are represented in our collection.

The Royal Bank understands the important role that art plays in enriching people's lives and invigorating the economy, and our commitment to these endeavours is real. We thank the artists represented here for the quality and diversity of their work. We also appreciate the months of hard work and dedication of the curators and many others involved in bringing this project together. We're proud to be supporting these people and these cities in such an exciting enterprise.

Bob Gunning
Director, Commercial Banking, East of Scotland
The Royal Bank of Scotland

6

Introduction

Any exhibition constrained in its focus by place and time risks suffering from a narrow frame of reference and a restricted field. Fortunately the focus of *Here + Now* has been a time of remarkable vitality in a place that has become the focus of much international attention, with exhibitions dedicated to Scottish Art taking place in cities from Reykjavik to Sydney. The exhibition benefits from and represents the diversity of work and the breadth of interests that exist in contemporary practice in Scotland. Bringing together works by over 60 artists, many of which have never previously been seen in Scotland, *Here + Now* acknowledges the undoubted achievements of Scotland's artists in recent years and aims to support their on-going success and progress, at an exciting time in the country's cultural and political history.

The years in question have seen extraordinary developments in visual art, from the initiatives of individual artists to the creation and development of major institutions. A voracious appetite for dialogue and a real interest in the world around us has resulted in the creation of some outstanding art. Drawing on references and materials from popular culture, the built environment, technological developments and many other sources, artists in Scotland have created works that encompass the beautiful, the strange, the humorous, the thought-provoking, the unsettling, the playful and the powerful, while happily using the familiar and the everyday.

Attempts have, of course, been made to define just what it is that connects loose groupings of artists and artworks such as that presented in this publication and the exhibition it accompanies, but as *Here + Now* demonstrates the only real defining feature is a pluralism of ideas, traditions and materials. Galleries have been tested by the diversity of media as disciplines have been seen to merge and grow in ambition like never before. Beyond the gallery, new audiences have embraced contemporary art in new environments. Just as Scotland can no longer be seen as a periphery of the international art world, art in Scotland has spread from established centres, transforming the cultural landscape. This has brought about the generation of centres of creativity in smaller cities, suburbs, housing estates and the rural environment in a series of memorably engaged public projects. Whilst such resolution by creators and commissioners is a phenomenon that is far from confined to Scotland, we can, perhaps for the first time, be seen to be providing models that are looked to from abroad.

Here + Now has involved the collaboration of five galleries in Aberdeen and Dundee, an ambitious project bringing together diverse spaces in two cities: Aberdeen Art Gallery, Dundee Contemporary Arts, Generator Projects, McManus Galleries and Peacock Visual Arts. An appropriately collaborative endeavour to explore a period that has seen artists organise exhibitions for one another through an expanding network of artist-run galleries and self-initiated projects. The years in question have been characterised by artists seeking, taking and making opportunities for dialogue and exchange at an international level.

Here + Now can only ever be a partial account of the past eleven years of art production in Scotland. This is not only because it cannot present all of the interesting artists working in Scotland (of whom there have been so many) but also because none of the artists presented has worked in a national vacuum defined by political borders. Many of the works presented have been made and exhibited alongside and sometimes in, or as the result of, collaboration with foreign peers. Just as artists from Scotland have exhibited extensively abroad, Scotland has reciprocated as major international figures have realised significant projects here (often at the invitation of the artists who are represented by this project).

Here + Now has been realised with the support and co-operation of many but we are particularly grateful to the Scottish Arts Council whose faith in the scale and significance of the exhibition at an early stage allowed it to progress from idea to reality. Such a large exhibition could not have been realised without the enthusiasm of many staff at all five of the participating organisations, and our thanks go to them. *Here + Now* and the previous exhibitions in the series have benefited from the support of the Scottish National Gallery of Modern Art, which has facilitated the loan of some significant works from the National Collection. We are also indebted to the several private and public collections that have lent works to the exhibition. In our post-devolution Scotland, it is particularly apt that we have been able to work with two prominent Scottish companies in The Royal Bank of Scotland and Scotland on Sunday, whose much-appreciated sponsorship has provided essential financial support. We are also grateful to The Hope Scott Trust for its support of this publication and to John Calcutt and Maria Lind for providing informative and considered essays. Finally, of course, our most profuse and sincere thanks must go to the artists, not only for the co-operation, support and patience that made the project possible, but most importantly for making Scottish art in the 1990s an excellent time and place.

Katrina M. Brown Curator
Rob Tufnell Assistant Curator
Dundee Contemporary Arts

There + Then John Calcutt

It was going to be the photograph to end all photographs, total killer-diller. A hot and sunny afternoon in New York City, September. Arnie was gone, his fast-mouthed inventory of Times Square ground rents still buzzing in our heads. The running stream of burning red letters on the Spectacolor display sped breaking news and falling share prices across the tall façade. It was the furthest thing from my mind at that moment. Arresting, then, across the traffic, above distracted heads: SCOTLAND VOTES FOR INDEPENDENCE. It took a minute or so to reappear, but the camera was patiently aimed, ready.

I should have known, I guess. I'm no camera person. Nevertheless, I sometimes pull that photograph out and gaze at it. When I look at the image of the thin horizontal strip strapped to the skinny building, its utter blankness, its complete blackness, seem to mock me. Fool, it says, for wanting to fix an image of history.

I think there is a complex allegory trying to find its way out here, but I don't know if I have the ingenuity and skill to guide it, or even if I want to. The elements I would have to marshal include: the relative accessibility of cosmopolitan experience; the political will of a nation; the crystallising power of imagery; the theory of 'decisive moments'; pride in an adopted national identity; belief in an imagined community of interests; the permanent possibility of failure and disappointment. I would have to say something about the phenomenon of coincidence and the enigma of 'being there' when 'it' happened. I would need to think about the curious entanglement of witnesses and events. In fact, I am disappointed by my own failure to work this potential allegory to its end. I sense it might help me understand something about the shape of Scottish art over the last decade or so. But something rises above the fancy twists and turns of this allegory: the fact that events in Scotland can register in the eyes of the world.

I arrived in Glasgow during the summer of 1987: new town, new job (at Glasgow School of Art). What did I know? Less than I thought. I brought the names Campbell, Howson, Currie and Wiszniewski with me, learned from the press, heard in the air. They were familiar, giving structure to an unfamiliar situation. Like a bat navigating the dark, I guessed that the echo of these names would help me judge distances, smooth the way, compensate for inadequate eyesight. Meanwhile. 1987: Craig Richardson and Douglas Gordon were among the group of students entering their final year in the Environmental Art department at Glasgow School of Art. David Harding was head of this newly established course, Sam Ainslie one of the tutors. This is how Harding remembers it:

'What amazed me was the sophistication of three or four of those particular students at that time. They seemed to have already articulated an opposition to painting, but particularly the figurative, expressionist, new painting of Wiszniewski, Campbell and these people. Now they had done this *in their first year*! […] To work with students who had such strongly held views – and *amazingly* coming out of West of Scotland comprehensives with a very developed view and knowledge of contemporary art practice – that was astonishing for me.'

What a wonderfully convenient coincidence for my account! At that very moment when I was using this group of painters as a reference point to enter a situation, the next generation of young artists was using them as a means of exit. The truth, of course, is rarely so neat. Harding continues: 'The other striking thing, of course, was that many of them painted! Douglas painted, Craig painted, Ross [Sinclair] did huge drawings and mainly did silkscreen printing. So they were using traditional means to move towards their ends. […] I'm not sure if they were clearly articulating at that time how they would move to where they were moving to …' Histories, nonetheless, are already being built on such uncertain foundations.

Anyone who attempts an historical account these days is obliged to offer disclaimers: me too. I live and work in Glasgow: it is from (t)here that I look around; it gives a particular angle to my perspective. It's where I know. It is also the place where I forget, misremember and misunderstand things, where I remain ignorant of so many events and activities. Nevertheless, it is a matter of plain fact that Glasgow has pretty much dominated the Scottish art scene since the late 1980s. The city is home to some of the most significant and influential institutions of this period. Let's see. Of the sixty-three artists included in this exhibition, around fifty attended Glasgow School of Art (GSA) at one time or another. Glasgow is also home to Transmission Gallery, established in 1983 by a group of culturally and politically disaffected 'cultural workers' – including John Rogan, Alistair Magee, Alastair Strachan, Michelle Baucke and Lesley Raeside – and now legendary among British artist-run organisations. (It might be interesting to count how many artists in this exhibition have served on its committee: around fifteen, I would guess.) Impossible to quantify, numerically or otherwise, would be the influence of exhibitions at the city's Centre for Contemporary Arts (formerly the Third Eye Centre) and Tramway, opened in 1990 to add substance to Glasgow's year-long reign as Cultural Capital of Europe.

Needless to say, the dominance of Glasgow throughout this period did not remain unchallenged. Edinburgh, one would think, should have had the edge. The nation's capital city, location of the country's national art collections, host to one of the world's greatest arts festivals, focus of the (admittedly limited) commercial art market in Scotland, home to Edinburgh College of Art, headquarters of the Scottish Arts Council. In short: the national centre of economic, cultural and political power. Yet simply to say that Edinburgh is conservative in its tastes and attitudes (albeit it as true as any generalisation may be) is probably not sufficient to account for the relative lack of an innovative, ambitious art scene in the late eighties and early

nineties. Perhaps, like me, it was looking in the wrong direction.

The mounting of *The Vigorous Imagination* at the Scottish National Gallery of Modern Art in 1987 had done much to canonise the work of a generation of broadly expressionist, predominantly figurative painters. Howson, Currie, Wiszniewski, Campbell, alongside others such as Gwen Hardie, Keith McIntyre, June Redfern and Stephen Conroy, were indelibly stamped with the imprimatur of the academy. Like it or not (and many of them did not) they had entered into official culture, assimilated into a recognisable and respectable tradition of Painting. They must have appeared to many as durable and bankable. The fact that they also seemed to represent a widespread national 'movement' (seven from Glasgow, six with Dundee connections, three from Edinburgh and one from Stirling) perhaps suggested that the future was assured, that there was no need to look any further.

But others, less convinced, maintained broader horizons. From the late seventies through the early eighties, for example, the New 57 Gallery (later absorbed in a somewhat drawn-out process by the Fruitmarket Gallery) had been staging a series of extraordinary exhibitions initiated by director Jim Birrell and board member Paul Stirton. These included the first British showings of Gordon Matta-Clark and Marcel Broodthaers, as well as shows by John Cage, Joseph Kosuth and Hans Haake – and early student outings for Campbell and Currie. The Collective Gallery was founded in 1983, set up on the lines of Transmission and some six months later by Edinburgh artists frustrated at a general lack of opportunity and interest in the city. It should be remembered, however, that for many young Scottish artists, including Kirsty McKee and Donald Urquhart (among others associated with the Collective Gallery) in Edinburgh and William (Billy) Clark and Malcolm Dickson (among others associated with Transmission) in Glasgow, the problem was not an exclusively cultural issue. The failure of the 1979 referendum to deliver a degree of political autonomy for Scotland came as a bitter blow to many. One of the upshots was a determination to at least establish a sense of artistic independence. Fuck London, they said, let's meet the world on our own terms. This is not the place to attempt anything other than a preliminary sketch of the developments occurring throughout this period, suffice it to say that the Edinburgh art scene limped through the eighties and early nineties. Its gradual revival owed much to the establishment of new institutions and galleries (The Fruitmarket Gallery, 1984; Inverleith House, 1986; Portfolio, 1988; Stills Gallery, 1977) and the appointment of knowledgeable and sympathetic directors and curators such as Sarah Monro (Collective Gallery) and Paul Nesbitt (Inverleith House). With the addition of recent establishments such as the Ingleby Gallery (1998), Sleeper (2000) and doggerfisher (2001), Edinburgh certainly leads the field in terms of exhibiting venues (public, independent and commercial), but it has yet to rival Glasgow as a centre of artistic production.

To the delight of many, the astonishment of others and the inevitable scepticism of a few, Dundee Contemporary Arts opened its doors in 1999, the presence of Secretary of State for Scotland, the late Donald Dewar, suggesting a new alliance between the newly confident powers of Scottish politics and Scottish art. A project that had been in the air since at least the mid-eighties, DCA sought to capitalise on the existing artistic energy of the city, an energy primarily focused on Duncan of Jordanstone College of Art & Design (DJCAD)[1], the Seagate Gallery and Dundee Printmakers

1. In 1992 at the time of the first Research Assessment Exercise for higher education institutions, Dundee's Duncan of Jordanstone College of Art had come top of the list of Scottish Art Schools, scoring 4 out of a possible 5. It was followed by Edinburgh (3), Gray's School of Art in Aberdeen (3) and, finally, Glasgow (2). The RAE has meant a shift in the criteria for funding higher education institutions towards research. The higher an institution scores – the greater the value attached to the public output of its staff in terms of exhibitions, publications and so on – the more money it receives in return.

Workshop. It was made possible not only by the enthusiasm and commitment of Dundee City Council, Dundee University and Dundee Contemporary Arts Ltd, but also by the award of £5.4 million from the Scottish Arts Council National Lottery Fund. The impact of these events was enormous: the development of contemporary art in Scotland could no longer be seen in terms of the Glasgow/Edinburgh axis. From the perspective of the central belt, Dundee suddenly didn't seem so far away. For some, of course, this came as little surprise. For those who had been teaching at DJCAD, such as Victoria Morton, Tracy Mackenna, Cathy Wilkes and Graham Fagen; for others associated with Steve Partridge's Television and Imaging department; for Deirdre MacKenna, who had been running the exhibitions programme at the college's Cooper Gallery since 1994, and for the artists of Generator, Dundee's own artist-run initiative (established in 1996), this must have seemed like long overdue recognition. The appointment of Andrew Nairne (ex-Third Eye Centre, ex-Scottish Arts Council) as director of DCA, along with curator Katrina Brown (ex-Transmission, Tramway and Tate Liverpool) and, latterly, Rob Tufnell guaranteed that the days of Dundee's marginalisation as a centre for contemporary art were over.

Scotland is not a big country, yet at times it might seem so. Aberdeen is roughly 130 miles from Edinburgh, 150 miles from Glasgow. When Matthew Dalziel and Louise Scullion decided to move to St Combs on the north-east coast between Peterhead and Fraserburgh they expected a certain amount of isolation. But they also knew that they were only an hour or so away from Aberdeen airport. They knew that fax, e-mail and the internet bring the world into the studio. And the north is hardly a cultural desert. With artists such as Jim Buckley and Jim Hamlyn (both involved in the artists group e@t) working alongside occasional visitors like Kenny Hunter and Claire Barclay at Gray's School of Art in Aberdeen, the region has its own scene. Aberdeen is home, for example, to Limousine Bull Artists Collective, the latest addition to those artist-run organisations so central to the development of innovative art practice in Scotland. Among

Dalziel + Scullion's closest neighbours were the freelance curator Iain Irving and the writer and critic Judith Finlay. Aberdeen Art Gallery also plays its part, participating in the last survey of Scottish art, *New Art in Scotland*, with the CCA, Glasgow in 1994, acquiring work by artists such as Alison Watt, Julie Roberts, Louise Hopkins and others – not to mention its involvement in the present exhibition and its forerunners. The ongoing Tyrebagger sculpture project located five miles to the north-west of the city in Kirkhill Forest has also been steadily developing since its inception in 1993. Co-ordinated by Edinburgh-based Art In Partnership (AIP) this ambitious scheme has facilitated the commissioning of important new work not only by Scottish artists such as Dalziel + Scullion and Donald Urquhart, but also by international figures such as Vong Phaophanit. AIP is also involved in the proposal for a site-specific work by Vito Acconci on Aberdeen seafront.

The Pier Arts Centre in Stromness, Orkney; Duff House in Banff (part of the National Galleries of Scotland); An Tuireann in Portree, Skye; An Lanntair in Stornoway: all of them play a significant role in helping to promote and encourage the development of new art throughout Scotland. Further south they are joined in this effort by the Crawford Arts Centre in St Andrews and the Changing Room in Stirling. Much of this work would be impossible without the financial support of the Scottish Arts Council (SAC). One of the remarkable features of the phenomenal success of recent Scottish art is that it has been achieved in

left Dave Allen and Louise Hopkins (pictured in front of Tony Cragg's *Congregation*, 1999) *Prime* Dundee Contemporary Arts 1999

right Jacqueline Donachie, Maria Lind, Katrina Brown, Calum Colvin, Roderick Buchanan and others at the opening of Dundee Contemporary Arts, 19 March 1999

the near total absence of a local market for the work. The Glasgow Art Fair first opened its doors in 1996 in an attempt to stimulate commercial interest, but the results so far are mixed. Apart from appearances by Transmission Gallery, The Modern Institute, Portfolio, Lapland and a few others, the vast majority of exhibitors remain resolutely safe and conventional. In this situation public funding for innovative art has assumed a major significance, the Scottish Arts Council spending £4.6 million on public art since 1995, monies often directed to projects initiated by agencies such as Glasgow-based Visual Art Projects, Edinburgh's Art In Partnership, as well as IPA and The Centre. The effects that this may have had upon the type of work produced by these artists are, however, yet to be explored. Money rarely arrives without strings attached, no matter how transpar-

left Jacqueline Donachie
Stars + Bars, Collective Gallery, Edinburgh 1997

right Jim Lambie *Voidoid*
Transmission Gallery, Glasgow 1999

ently. What is evident, however, is that much of the public art resulting from these projects is intent on exploring issues, processes and situations, rather than merely providing decorative objects. Two factors may be relevant here: the legacy of attitudes to public art encouraged on the Environmental Art course at GSA; and the lack of a commercial art market, leading many artists to focus on art as a process of investigation, rather than as a pragmatic means of financial reward.

SAC funds arrive in a variety of guises – and there never seems to be enough. Nevertheless, the influx of cash into the SAC National Lottery Capital Fund since March 1995 has amounted to over £94 million. Among the results of this financial windfall – apart from the funding of public art mentioned above – were the building of Dundee Contemporary Arts; the major redevelopment of Tramway and the Centre for Contemporary Arts in Glasgow; the refurbishment of Stills Gallery and the Collective Gallery in Edinburgh. As far as Glasgow is concerned, the long-term effects of this process are yet to be counted. Despite the fact that both Tramway and the CCA attempted to maintain their exhibition programmes by 'borrowing' other spaces whilst their galleries were closed for building work (CCA reopens in October 2001) their prolonged closure slowed down artistic activity in the city for the duration. Momentum dissipated, focus was lost. As far as 'major' shows were concerned, attention shifted to Edinburgh and Dundee.

Although I have been concentrating here on some of the local and national conditions under which most of the art in this exhibition has been produced, it would be wrong to assume that its concerns, interests and ambitions are parochial or chauvinistic. One of the great strengths of this art is the confidence with which it assumes its place in the international arena. Many of these artists are actually far better known (and respected) abroad than at home. This determination to expand beyond national borders, to engage in an international exchange of ideas and experiences was clearly evident in *Windfall*, an exhibition organised by Glasgow artists in 1991 and billed as '25 artists representing 8 European countries.' Ross Sinclair's essay for the catalogue of this show offers the clearest, most forceful account of many of the attitudes informing this project:

'Artist initiatives are a valuable way of demystifying the business of art. They promote a sharing of information, skills and experiences while also nurturing relationships between artists that can often become fertile breeding grounds for a horizontal and organically developing infrastructure of cultural activity. They often embrace a desire to communicate with that great unfashionable and unknown quantity, the general public. [...]

What has finally been exorcised is a feeling evident in years gone by that coming from Glasgow, or Belfast or any other city meant having a chip on your shoulder, feeling short changed because you weren't born in New York or London. What is happening now is active – not re-active… Past prejudices have been shrugged off and a passionate internationalism is being embraced.'

Contact with the international scene is thus vital, and it is no surprise to find that in May 2001 alone the SAC awarded thirteen small grants to representatives of the various sectors of the art world to support travel to the Venice Biennale (and the Basle art fair, in some cases). Another recent addition to the financial support available to artists[2] comes in the form of the annual SAC Creative Scotland Awards, fourteen grants of £25,000 each distributed across all the art forms. Recent recipients of visual art awards include Roderick Buchanan and Nathan Coley, although artists of this younger generation were passed over in favour of more established figures in the first year of the scheme's existence.

Lest this appear like a eulogy for the Scottish Arts Council, it should also be pointed out that many of its decisions, many of its policies are hotly contested, openly challenged. Anyone who thinks the Scottish art world is one big happy family is sadly misguided. If I have given the impression that everything is laid on for these artists, then that too must be corrected. Virtually all the achievements that this exhibition invites us to consider have been hard won. And the battles are still being fought. At both local and national governmental level officialdom, it seems, simply will not recognise the success that surrounds it. Glasgow's Gallery of Modern Art continues to lack any representation of the work of the city's many highly successful artists. Douglas Gordon's receipt of the Lord Provost's Award from Glasgow City Council in 1998 – two years after his success in the Turner Prize – was a token of recognition as belated as it was surprising. Ross Birrell's recent request to work as artist-in-residence at the new Scottish Parliament building

2. Over and above the on-going funds used to support the year-in, year-out running of studios (e.g. WASPS) and workshops, which provide a constant underpinning of exhibiting opportunity and technical provision that contributes significantly to the distinctive characteristics of the Scottish situation at grassroots level.

left Hayley Tompkins and Cathy Wilkes pictured at *Add Night to Night*, The Showroom, London 1998

right Callum Innes in his studio, Edinburgh

was finally rejected (along with Nathan Coley, Chad McCail, Jacqueline Donachie and many others, Birrell is one of the official artists during the Year of the Artist, 2000/1). Is it any wonder that Transmission Gallery (followed by the Collective Gallery and, more recently, Generator and Limousine Bull) sought a solution in artist-run organisations? Is it any wonder that friendships formed in early adversity still hold firm? When artists have to fight for what they believe in – when they understand that something is at stake in their endeavour – is it any wonder they often look askance at those who chose a different route, a different set of investments?

Curators and critics are often maligned, but they have an important role to play in a situation as intellectually, ideologically and geographically fractured as the one I am outlining here. A great deal of this work may have originated from the lonely, obsessive pursuits of bedroom culture (the interest in popular culture, subculture, music and so on which is evident in the work of Jim Lambie, Ross Sinclair, Dave Allen, Lucy McKenzie and others). Many of the ideas and attitudes embodied in it may have been tested and developed in bar-room arguments and late night kitchen discussions. But unless it somehow engages with wider public discourse and socio-cultural concerns it is condemned to pointlessness. (Pointlessness may be its legitimate concern, but it only becomes significantly pointless when it asks for that pointlessness to be publicly considered.) Curators and critics are the agents of such discourse, mediators who pull the work into the public domain. The problem, of course, is that curators and critics have their own agendas. But Scotland, it seems to me, has been extremely fortunate in terms of curators. In certain notable instances those curators have themselves been artists. In Glasgow the committee members of Transmission offer a good example, as does the often forgotten David McMillan, one of the prime movers behind the seminal *Windfall* show in 1991 and instigator of Breathe (later Intermedia, originally a temporary gallery project in the Merchant City area of the city). Working under the title 'Charisma', Lucy McKenzie and Keith Farquhar have also instigated interesting curatorial projects recently. As far as professional curators are concerned, it is safe to say that in the hands of Andrew Nairne (Third Eye Centre/CCA/DCA), Nicola White (CCA/Tramway – where she commissioned Douglas Gordon's *24 Hour Psycho*), Charles Esche (Tramway, The Modern Institute) and Francis McKee (CCA) new Scottish art has been actively supported in certain major Glasgow venues throughout the 1990s and beyond. The names of Sarah Munro and Paul Nesbitt in Edinburgh have already been mentioned, as have those of Katrina Brown, Rob Tufnell and Deirdre MacKenna in Dundee and Iain Irving in Aberdeen-shire. To them might be added Toby Webster (The Modern Institute), Graeme Murray (Fruitmarket Gallery), Keith Hartley (Scottish National Gallery of Modern Art), Claudia Zeiske (Duff House), Neil Firth (Pier Arts Centre), Kate Tregaskis (Stills Gallery until 2001), Jackie Shearer (ex-Fotofeis and Changing Room), Alexia Holt (Tramway) and many more.

As far as critics and critical debate are concerned, it is a slightly different story. There are, it is true, some very interesting writers around, among them artists such as Ross Sinclair, Graham Fagen and Ross Birrell (plus many more, such as Richard Wright and Douglas Gordon who can write with the best but who, for various reasons, don't). The problem really concerns outlets for critical writing. Since the final demise of *Alba* in 1992 Scotland has not managed to establish a journal or magazine dedicated to critical commentary on contemporary visual art. *Transcript* (launched in 1994), issuing from DJCAD, has been recently dormant, its contribution sadly missed – as is that of its co-founder and co-editor, the late Alan Woods. The latest incarnation of *Variant: cross-currents in culture* (edited by William Clark and Leigh French since 1996) is intellectually tough and politically sharp, but it seems, unlike its earlier existence under the editorship of Malcolm Dickson (1985–1993), to avoid contemporary art as a matter of principle. Long may it thrive, but it needs company. *Product. popartpolitics* came out of

left Nathan Coley, *A Public Announcement*, The Changing Room, Stirling 1998

right Audience at first showing of Roderick Buchanan's *Out*, Dundee Contemporary Arts 2000

Edinburgh in December 1999, but addresses itself to a general readership. *292: essays in visual culture* was founded by Andrew Patrizio at Edinburgh College of Art in 1999 and its unique combination of scholarship, literary ambition and artists' pages looks very promising. Photography and sculpture are catered for by, respectively, *Portfolio* (edited by Gloria Chambers from Portfolio gallery) and *Sculpture Matters* (first published by the Scottish Sculpture trust in June 1997), but there are no equivalents for other media. There have been some valuable publishing initiatives from artists (including *StopStop*, *British Mythic* and *atopia*) but, apart from Alec Finlay's Pocketbook series and other projects from his Morning Star Press, these are generally sporadic and/or patchily distributed. That leaves newspapers and listings magazines, neither of them the ideal place to develop a substantial critical practice. This is a great shame. With writers as inventive and knowledgeable as Neil Mulholland, Will Bradley, Jenny Brownrigg and, especially, the prodigious and highly respected Francis McKee there is no shortage of talent.

I began with a story – an unresolved allegory – because I wanted to avoid producing a mere list of individuals, events and institutions. I chose not to discuss works of art because I wanted to concentrate upon some of the conditions that made such work possible. I end in defeat. I produced a list, but it is far from complete. Its many omissions include the impact of Pavel Büchler's brief but eventful period as head of Fine Art at Glasgow School of Art, Amanda Catto's supportive work at SAC, Sam Ainslie's indefatigable enthusiasm on all fronts, especially as head of the MFA course at GSA. I didn't get around to discussing *Fotofeis*, the short-lived national bi-annual festival of photography (1993, 1995 and 1997). Or *Lux Europe*, a festival of public art featuring work using the medium of light to celebrate the meeting of European Heads of Government summit in Edinburgh, 1992. Or the impact of The Modern Institute, set up in 1996. Or such major celebrations of contemporary international art as *Plano XXI* (curated by António Regoin, Glasgow, 2000) and *Vivre sa Vie* (Tanya Leighton, Glasgow and Edinburgh, 2001). I may also have given the impression that the work in this exhibition (as well as much other significant

left Toby Paterson and Jim Lambie pictured at The Modern Institute, Glasgow

right Martin Boyce at Roderick Buchanan's *Players*, Dundee Contemporary Arts 2000

3. In an interview with Douglas
Gordon as yet unpublished.

work produced during this period but not included) is simply
the passive product of a given situation. Not so. The
influential Swiss curator Hans Ulrich Obrist's much-quoted
summary of the situation as 'the Glasgow miracle'[3] was
both right and wrong: right in that he had identified something extraordinary taking place in this country; wrong
insofar as it was no miracle. Miracles are supernatural
phenomena, they occur inexplicably. The achievements
registered in this exhibition were born of relentless effort
and persistence, frequently in the face of scepticism and
doubt. They are the products of optimism and confidence,
often nurtured by support and encouragement, sometimes
dented by rejection and neglect. I would like to talk about
seriousness, their sheer variety, their often staggering
incisiveness – but that's another story.

John Calcutt is an art critic and lecturer in Historical and Critical Studies
at Glasgow School of Art

Notes on Contemporary Art in a Relative Periphery

Maria Lind

Some earn exorbitant money from it, others are impover-
ished because of it. Books are written about it and confer-
ences are staged. During recent years thousands and
thousands of people in various parts of the world have taken
to the streets to demonstrate against it. People can even,
we now know, be killed by the police for protesting against
it. I am referring of course to 'globalisation', an amoebic
concept yet one currently on practically everyone's lips.
With an undoubted potential to mobilise more and larger
street protests than any other contemporary issue, it is a
phenomenon of which most are aware but few can explain.
Seldom is it specified exactly how, when and where it takes
place.

If we nevertheless try to approach one aspect of this
unwieldy burning issue, we should ask ourselves: to what
extent is globalisation equal to standardisation, making
everywhere the same? How much does it contribute to
diversity, to localising processes? The Indian-born anthro-
pologist, Arjun Appadurai, now resident in the US, writes
about how the discussions of the homogenising effects of
globalisation often quite rightly deal with Americanisation
and commodification, with McDonald's as a prime example.
But what about the other side of the coin: what is happening
regarding local indiginisation and processing – cultural
cannibalisation? He points out how music, for example, in
different parts of the world is transformed and 'made local',
and notes that in a place like Sri Lanka, 'Indianisation' is a
greater problem than Americanisation, as is 'Japanification'
for Koreans.

It was not a revelation, but it was a discovery, and a forma-
tive one – a sudden awareness of the art scene in Glasgow.
It was 1994 and for some time I had been watching the

work of a number of artists, all of whom it turned out, worked in Scotland. Finally, I realised it was not enough to see a single work in an exhibition and to read articles in magazines. I had to go to Scotland not only to extend my knowledge of these artists (and hopefully others), but also to appreciate something of the situation that had obviously produced such good art. With his usual generosity, a Scottish-friendly but London-based artist equipped me with some useful telephone numbers, and off I went by train from London to Glasgow, via Llandudno in Wales and the exhibition *Riviera*,[1] where many of the Scottish artists I was interested in were just then. This was the first of many trips to Scotland, the first of many encounters, conversations and collaborations there and elsewhere, which have not only influenced how I look at art and curating but has also affected me – I dare say – as an individual.

1. At the Oriel Mostyn Gallery, Llandudno in September – October 1994, *Riviera* included works by Christine Borland, Roderick Buchanan, Nathan Coley, Annete Heyer, Jim Hamlyn. Craig Richardson and Julie Roberts.

So-called 'area studies' are passé in the academic world. To use a geographically defined area as the basic premise for one's studies is considered a simplification. Nevertheless, people like Arjun Appadurai continue to insist on the need for such studies. Although they may be a double-edged sword, not only reducing non-western cultures to their bare essences but also used to control them (as Edward Said and others have shown) they are nonetheless a counterbalance to cultural vanity and self-interest. They give room to the Other, to foreign languages and other points of view and ways of seeing; they are 'a salutary reminder that globalisation itself is a deeply historical, uneven and even localising process'. In the context of art, geographically based exhibitions may be compared to area studies but to that part which is primary research: the first step in the processing of material. This 'primary curating' carries some of the same risks as area studies but also some of the same advantages. When it is carried out on home ground, it can, in the best instances, become a useful exercise in looking anew at one's own house and neighbours.

By now there have been numerous exhibitions and projects discussing art in Scotland in the 1990s as seen from elsewhere and there are numerous catalogue texts and other articles that endeavour to tell 'Scottish Contemporary Art – The Story'. Among the points made in such texts that I tend to agree with is the belief that the educational infrastructure has played a crucial role. The much-quoted notion that 'the context is half the work' continues to reverberate. But then again, other artists cherish the qualities and associations of various materials and use them as their starting point. For just as one can attempt to discern common denominators in the work, there are also distinct differences – this is not one big happy family. That the work has, according to one writer, 'entered the realm of the psyche' does, however, seem important in many cases, and the occasional reference to a 'poetic conceptualism' is one of the more useful terms to describe much of this work. Looking through the various texts telling The Story, it is remarkable how many of them are quite personal; writers including anecdotes and other personalised comments, something no doubt connected to the fact that social, discursive interaction lies at the heart of the approach of many of these artists.

Any such history has to acknowledge the extent to which artist-run spaces and initiatives have played a part in forming the scene. Most of these artists have experience mediating their own work as well as the work of others: they have worked on committees, they have put together exhibition programmes, repainted galleries, licked stamps, applied for money and installed work together with other artists. Some have written extensively on contemporary art. In between some have played football together (the men, that is) and met in the pub. And they have talked, and talked and talked (and it can take some time for an outsider to penetrate the accent). International contacts have been there from very early on, often since art school, and early on at Transmission Gallery, where they mixed local art with globally famous players. So, it is not surprising that when they themselves began to exhibit internationally, they did not go via the traditional political and economic route – that is, via London – but direct: Scotland to the rest of the world.

Art in Scotland, Scandinavia, Eastern Europe, Canada, Mexico and other locales has long been treated like the poor country cousin of the true metropolitan centres of Paris, London, New York and so on. It has been in the family of the mainstream, but considered rather unsophisticated and a little embarrassing. It has shared certain frames of reference with the big boys in the centre of the world, but not all of them and their dialects have been difficult to understand. At the same time, art from these areas hasn't been sufficiently foreign and exotic to be grouped together in exhibitions like *Magiciens de la terre*[2] – it has not been 'other' enough. In today's 'glocal' situation, however, the traditional centres have an increasingly difficult time upholding this picture of their cousins. The ability to read each other's work is great (whether admitted or not) when art demonstrates common characteristics in widely diverse places, because of, or thanks to, the common references that result from globalisation. In conjunction with this, art also often reveals special features – specific and local subjects, methods and attitudes.

2. At the Centre Georges Pompidou, Paris in 1989.

It is also said that many smaller centres have replaced the large few: that Glasgow, Copenhagen, Vilnius, Ljubljana and Vancouver have acquired a new importance. This is true, but rather than see it as a paradise of equality, I would retain and reformulate the older paradigm of centre-periphery that makes visible the geopolitical power struc-ture, which, despite all, still prevails, not least economically. The fundamental centre-periphery structure remains, but some of the peripheries are less peripheral and the centres are less central – everything has become relative. Just as the private, the female and the emotional can no longer so simply be subordinated to the public, male and the intellec-tual. One may wonder if this is not advantageous: we can call Scotland a relative centre but it is more of a relative periphery – a place situated geographically on the edge but with constant contact with both other relative peripheries and relative centres. Which at the same time is self-aware and able to make use of the advantage of standing a little to one side. Perhaps the scenario would have looked different if instead of McDonald's, a 'Dundee Burgers' chain had survived the 1950s to win international domination in the quickest growing global industry and therefore one of the most powerful shapers of taste, as well as other habits – fast food.

I have often wondered why it is that the quality of Scottish art of the last fifteen years is so high, for I have never experienced, or heard about, any other context that has produced so many outstanding artists. Over the years these artists' work continues to captivate me; I am curious about what they are doing – sometimes I am also puzzled and sceptical – but always curious. Is it the same hard-to-define dynamic that also lies behind the difficulty in explaining why one class in the same school with the same teacher functions better than another? Or why one team functions better than another? Or does this quality emanate from its Scottish heritage, with roots in David Hume's empiricism and Adam Smith's moral philosophy? And by extension, the desire to discuss constantly, to prod and poke, to mull over their own and others' practices, politics and sport, philosophy and films, history and fashion? Does it lie in part in the Scots' experience of being absorbed by a greater, more dominant nation? One constant element in the various artists' work, interests and means of expression, seems to be the ability to follow through consistently what has been undertaken, whether an idea or a material association. Perhaps what we have in contemporary art in Scotland is an unusually fruitful case study, in which the Enlightenment dream of combining the general and the specific is materialised.

Maria Lind is a Curator at the Moderna Museet, Stockholm.

Artists in the exhibition

Dave Allen

Claire Barclay

Emily Bates

Anne Bevan

Christine Borland

Martin Boyce

Roderick Buchanan

Jim Buckley

Paul Carter

Nathan Coley

Alan Currall

Matthew Dalziel and Louise Scullion

Jacqueline Donachie

Chris Evans

Graham Fagen

Keith Farquhar

Moyna Flannigan

Douglas Gordon

Kate Gray

Kevin Henderson

Annette Heyer

Steve Hollingsworth

Louise Hopkins

Kenny Hunter

Callum Innes

Iain Kettles and Susie Hunter

Jim Lambie

Tracy Mackenna and Edwin Janssen

Chad McCail

Lucy McKenzie

Wendy McMurdo

Janice McNab

Alan Michael

Andrew Miller

Victoria Morton

Toby Paterson

Mary Redmond

Carol Rhodes

Craig Richardson

Julie Roberts

David Shrigley

Ross Sinclair

Stephanie Smith and Eddie Stewart

Bryndis Snæbjörnsdóttir

Simon Starling

Joanne Tatham and Tom O'Sullivan

James Thornhill

Graeme Todd

Hayley Tompkins

Donald Urquhart

Clara Ursitti

Alison Watt

Cathy Wilkes

Michael Wilkinson

Richard Wright

Dave **Allen**

Born in Glasgow in 1963, Dave Allen studied on the MA course at Glasgow School of Art between 1992 and 1994. Allen had his first solo exhibition at Transmission Gallery, Glasgow in 1990 where he was also a member of the committee. He has participated in several important group exhibitions involving artists from Scotland including *Windfall '91*, Glasgow, *Sawn-Off* in Stockholm, 1996 and *Circles #4* at ZKM, Karlsruhe, 2001. The Showroom Gallery, London will present a solo show in 2001. Allen is currently based in Berlin.

Dave Allen's practice highlights the numerous points of contact between art production and music. Allen is best known for a series of transcriptions of rock songs for the amateur musician, which he presents as instructions on canvas. Two screenprints, *Stairway to Heaven / Highway to Hell* present Led Zeppelin and AC/DC's infamous anthems in an ironic pairing.

Interpretation of 'Prélude à l'Après-midi d'un Faune' (1892–94) by Claude Debussy, arranged without key signature for the untrained pianist, version II, 2000, takes the piece credited as the first example of Modern music and introduces a spirit of amateurism. Debussy's work is simplified and presented hand-written on a wall. We associate such a do-it-yourself attitude with 1970's Punk Rock; perhaps the ultimate result of the movement Debussy began. *Version II* is a re-writing by Allen of an earlier attempt at the piece that was first exhibited at The Modern Institute, Glasgow, in 1999. **RT**

Interpretation of 'Prélude à l'Après-midi d'un Faune' (1892–94) by Claude Debussy, arranged without key signature for the untrained pianist, version II 2000
marker pen on paper · courtesy the artist

Claire **Barclay**

Born in Paisley in 1968, Claire Barclay studied in the Environmental Art Department at Glasgow School of Art, where she also obtained an MA in 1993. Her first solo exhibition was at Transmission Gallery, Glasgow in 1994. She was selected for the Scottish Arts Council's Australia residency in 1995–96. Her work has been included in many group exhibitions in the UK, Europe and Australia. In 2000 Barclay realised solo projects at The Showroom, London and the Moderna Museet, Stockholm. She is currently a Fellow at Glasgow School of Art and continues to be based in Glasgow.

Using diverse materials, Claire Barclay's sculptures and objects tend to coalesce around a relationship between the natural and the artificial. Many of her works in recent years have combined elements of slick, machine-finished materials such as aluminium with those that are more craft-like and hand-made, such as sewn fabric and hand-cut paper. All her works betray a fascination for the materials with which she works, allowing an intriguing relationship to emerge between the elements. 'While there is always a concept behind the work its actual form comes out of the 'play' with materials and my response to them' (CB).

For the exhibition *Girls' High* at the Old Fruitmarket in Glasgow in 1996 Barclay used the delicate, tactile and decorative qualities of a black feather boa to express the dynamics of the architecture of the disused and run-down space, extending it from floor to ceiling and attaching it to the ground by means of an immaculate white leather strip and steel fixings. Her recent works have continued to suggest a range of oppositional relationships, between delicacy and strength, the urban and the rural, the artificial and the natural, the mass-produced and the hand-crafted. Though such tensions are undoubtedly embedded in the objects with which she presents us, these works retain an ability to speak directly to our senses as well as our intellect. They rely on our innate ability to relate to materials. **KB**

REFERENCES

Homemaking, Moderna Museet, Stockholm, 2000

Take to the Ground, The Showroom, London, 2000

Work from **Take to the Ground**
(at The Showroom, London) 2000
turned aluminium and pony skin · courtesy the artist

Emily **Bates**

Born in Basingstoke, 1970, Emily Bates studied Textiles at Glasgow School of Art graduating in 1993. She has exhibited extensively in Britain and internationally in group shows including *Addressing the Century: 100 Years of Art and Fashion* at the Hayward Gallery, London, in 1998, and at the Kunstmuseum, Wolfsburg, in 1999. In 1997 she was awarded the Scottish Arts Council's Amsterdam Studio Residency. In 2000 she completed artist residencies at The Pier Arts Centre, Stromness and the Nordiska Akvarellmuseet in Sweden. She currently lives and works in Amsterdam.

Emily Bates is best known for a series of oversized dresses constructed from spun and knitted human hair that she has described as 'impossible dresses'. Works such as *Sibilla*, 1997, reveal Bates' interests in the mythological importance attached to hair and also in the way in which women express themselves through their hair and clothing.

Subsequent photographic works have presented combinations of hair and clothes worn within surreal, domestic narratives. Bates' most recent series of works, collectively titled *Re-habitation*, continue these themes in evocative locations. She describes the images as 'both familiar and unknown, fake and real, staged and intuitive'. *Cave*, 2000, depicts the artist wearing a beard fashioned from her own hair set within the Orkadian landscape. **RT**

Sibilla 1997
spun and woven human hair · courtesy the artist

Anne **Bevan**

Born in Orkney in 1965, Anne Bevan studied at Edinburgh College of Art and Edinburgh University, completing her studies in 1998. Solo exhibitions of her work have been presented at the Collective Gallery, Edinburgh, the Pier Arts Centre, Stromness and most recently the Fruitmarket Gallery, Edinburgh, where her *undercover* project was exhibited in 2000. She now lives and works in Edinburgh.

Bevan's mixed media works excavate the often invisible or at least ignored structures that surround our daily lives. She exposes and reveals spaces, systems, routes and movements normally unseen by us, but which are fundamental to the everyday environment we inhabit. Writer Murdo Macdonald has described her work as 'Traces of movement held in space'.

Her interest in underground spaces and hidden water systems was the origin of the *undercover* project in 2000. The project began as an investigation of 'what lies under the manhole covers in our streets' and the exhibited works resulted from a period of research with East of Scotland Water. The video projections, images, cast objects and sounds presented in the exhibition together question our assumption of water as a natural and plentiful element, rather than the highly controlled commodity as which it exists in our environment. *covered (leaks)* is a series of tiny metal forms, residues of water escaping from its intended and controlled course. 'The stalactites were picked like snapped shots from the weeping tunnel ceilings of the reservoir' (Brian Hand in *Pipelines*). Typically, with these works Bevan finds the delicate and the unexpected in the incidental and the industrial. **KB**

REFERENCES

Lifting Light, Pier Arts Centre, Stromness, Orkney, 1997

Pipelines with Janice Galloway, Fruitmarket Gallery, Edinburgh, 2000

covered (leaks) 2000
silver electroformed lime stalactites, glass shelf · courtesy the artist

Christine **Borland**

Born in Darvel, Ayrshire in 1965, Christine Borland studied in the Environmental Art Department at Glasgow School of Art and later obtained an MA from the University of Ulster in Belfast in 1988. Borland was a committee member of Transmission Gallery from 1989 to 1991 and took part in the exhibitions *Self-Conscious State* at the Third Eye Centre, Glasgow in 1990 and *Guilt by Association* at the Irish Museum of Modern Art, Dublin in 1992. Her first solo exhibition, *From Life,* for which she collaborated with forensic scientists, was presented at Tramway, Glasgow in 1994 and subsequently at Kunst Werke in Berlin. She has also participated in a number of important international exhibitions, such as the 1995 Venice Biennale, *Sculpture Projects, Münster* in 1997 and *Manifesta 2* in Luxembourg in 1998. In 1998–99 she was the subject of a major retrospective exhibition at De Appel, Amsterdam, the Museum für Gegenwartskunst, Zürich and the Fundaçao Serralves, Porto. In 1999 an exhibition of Borland's newly commissioned work was presented at Dundee Contemporary Arts.

REFERENCES

Progressive Disorder, Dundee Contemporary Arts / Book Works, London, 2001

The Dead Teach the Living, De Appel, Amsterdam / Fundaçao Serralves, Oporto / Migros Museum, Zürich, 2001

From work in the early 1990s, which first explored the fields of forensics and criminology, to more recent work with human genetics, Borland's work consistently challenges our notions of the division between art and science, between emotion and logic. It encourages an awareness of the relationship between the observer and the object of study.

English Family China was made for the *Artranspennine* exhibition at Tate Liverpool in 1998. The starting point for the piece was a visit to Liverpool Museum, where Borland saw the remarkable collection of commemorative bowls given to ships on their maiden voyages, ships that were trading in produce from Africa and the Far East as well as in slaves. The bowls were symbolic not only of Liverpool's former prominence as a trading port but also of the significance of the city and surrounding area as a major producer of bone china during the 18th century, when import from the Orient was banned. The china tableware was decorated with faux oriental designs, a style often referred to as 'Spode china' after Josiah Spode, one of the leading makers in England. Borland's project brought together these strands with her on-going interest in how meaning is invested in and lost from objects, including human remains.

The bone china skulls, made in Buchlyvie in Scotland, are grouped in five 'families' each designated with its own pattern, using centuries-old techniques to subtly evoke contemporary issues of cloning and genetic engineering, issues which have become central to Borland's most recent works. KB

English Family China 1998
hand painted bone china · courtesy the artist and National Museums and Galleries on Merseyside (Walker Art Gallery)

Martin **Boyce**

Born in Hamilton in 1967, Martin Boyce studied in the Environmental Art Department and on the MA course at Glasgow School of Art, which he completed in 1997. His first solo exhibition was at the Agency, London, in 1995. He has participated in several important group exhibitions involving artists from Scotland including *Windfall '91*, Glasgow, *Nettverk – Glasgow* in Oslo, 1998, *Open Country* in Lausanne and *Circles #4* at ZKM, Karlsruhe in 2001. In 1999 he had a solo exhibition at the Fruitmarket Gallery, Edinburgh. Boyce participated in the *British Art Show 5* in 2000 and in the same year he was short-listed for the inaugural Beck's Futures Prize. 2002 sees a solo show at Tramway, Glasgow. He lives and works in Glasgow.

Martin Boyce's work is concerned with the way in which signs and symbols change over the course of time. Boyce draws points of reference from art history, cinema, design and literature. Work made in recent years has focussed on design from the 1950's; furniture and graphics produced at the height of the Modern movement when societies were perhaps more optimistic about the future.

Boyce has re-made Modern furniture designed by Charles and Ray Eames to reflect contemporary pessimism. He has also made a number of large scale wall drawings based upon the graphic work of the designer Saul Bass taken from the opening credits of Alfred Hitchcock's *North by Northwest*, 1959. Boyce presents this stylised graphic as a looming presence articulating contemporary urban paranoia.

Broken Sledge (Forever), 1992, comprises a child's sledge bearing the hopeful legend 'Forever'. The sledge is broken, contradicting its inscription. The work is inspired by the sledge, bearing the inscription 'Rosebud', that features in Orson Welles' film *Citizen Kane*, 1941. RT

REFERENCE

Martin Boyce, Fruitmarket Gallery, Edinburgh, 2000

Broken Sledge (Forever) 1992
broken sledge · courtesy the artist and The Modern Institute

Roderick **Buchanan**

Born in Glasgow in 1965, Buchanan studied in the Environmental Art Department at Glasgow School of Art and later for an MA at the University of Ulster in Belfast in 1989–90. He was a committee member of Transmission Gallery, Glasgow from 1990–1992. He participated in the exhibitions *Self-Conscious State* at the Third Eye Centre, Glasgow in 1990 and *Guilt by Association* at the Irish Museum of Modern Art, Dublin in 1992. His first solo show was of the photographic installation *Work in Progress* at Tramway in 1995. Buchanan's work with video, photography, sculpture and text has been exhibited widely in Europe, Australia and the U.S. and was included in the 1999 and 2001 Venice Biennale exhibitions. He was awarded the first Beck's Futures Prize at the ICA, London in 2000 and later that year Dundee Contemporary Arts presented his first major solo exhibition, *Players*. He was the recipient of a Creative Scotland Award in 2001.

REFERENCE

Players, Dundee Contemporary Arts, 2000

Buchanan's works with both photography and video can be seen as contemporary versions of the most traditional of genres in art: portraiture and landscape, in as much as they ask us to explore how we go about investing character in people and places. Formal sports and informal games have featured regularly in Buchanan's works of recent years. These are examined not for the competition itself, but to assess how our recreational activities – what we do with time that is our own – express identity. Previous works have used everything from an informal children's game to the most commercialised and formalised of sports – the football World Cup and the Tour de France. Buchanan's interest is not in the games themselves, but in issues of race, nationality, culture, identity, aspiration and allegiance that surround the fields of play.

A recurrent aspect of Buchanan's work has been the abstraction of physical elements of formal, controlled spaces, allowing an unusual encounter with supposedly familiar spaces, such as his *Full Scale Premiere League Goal Mouth*, 1992, a simple white line along the gallery floor delineating the area described. His ability to abstract the extraordinary from the everyday is evident also in his more recent video *Endless Column*, 1999. The piece uses TV coverage of international rugby matches, from which Buchanan has simply edited together footage of the moment when each country's national anthems is sung by the respective teams prior to the match. The silent work is a continuous loop, showing us one national team after another, edited together in such a way as you have to watch carefully for the shift – or can you tell by the players' very appearance? As with so many of Buchanan's works, *Endless Column* immediately prompts an awareness of our attempts to interpret appearance. KB

Endless Column 1999
video still · courtesy the artist and Lisson Gallery

Jim **Buckley**

Born in Cork in 1957, Jim Buckley studied at Crawford School of Art, Cork. He participated in the multi-site *Kunst Europa* exhibition in Germany in 1991. His solo exhibition *Access* was presented at the Collins Gallery, Glasgow, Tullie House, Carlisle and Gracefield Arts Centre, Dumfries in 1992–3. He has realised a number of public projects in Britain and abroad. Buckley is a lecturer in Sculpture at Gray's School of Art in Aberdeen. Buckley is currently on a studio residency in New York, where he is undertaking research into public art projects in the city.

In the early 1990s, Jim Buckley's interest as a sculptor in the creation of interior, public spaces led him to develop a series of works which appear as wall mounted boxes, simple in form but suggesting the exterior of buildings. The front-most surface of each box is punctured by a small glass view-finder, just like those to be found in homes and hotel rooms, inviting the viewer to look inside. On pressing the accompanying timer switch to activate the light necessary to see inside, the viewer discovers a world in miniature, grand architectural spaces devoid of any human presence. The titles communicate a sense of protection – *Asylum*, *Refuge*, *Ark* – sustained by the discovery of the internal spaces which convey Buckley's interest in 'the creation of a space to feel comfortable in, a shelter from the world outside'. **KB**

'Neither sensible nor sensationalist, real nor fantastic, inspection involves private feelings of surprise, delight, intrigue or unease as we imagine ourselves existing within the bizarre echo of such isolation.'
Paul Nesbitt in *Jim Buckley: Access*, 1992

REFERENCE

Access, Collins Gallery, Glasgow, 1992

Interim 1994 (external and internal views)
stainless steel, brass, glass, plywood, paper, perspex · courtesy the artist

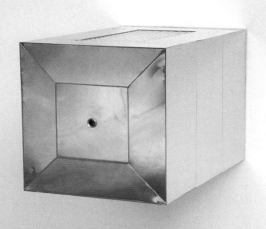

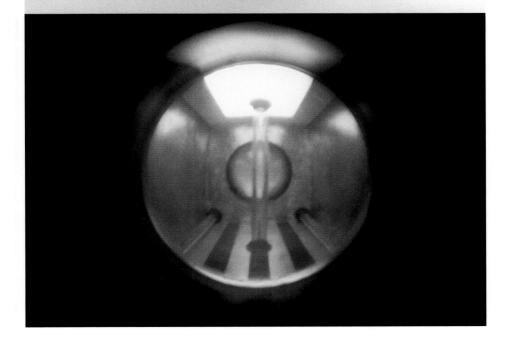

Paul **Carter**

Born in Edinburgh in 1970, Paul Carter
studied Sculpture at Edinburgh School
of Art and on the MA course at Glasgow
School of Art, 1993–1995. His first
significant solo exhibition was in 1998
at the Collective Gallery, Edinburgh. He
has exhibited extensively in Britain and
in 2001 he completed a major public art
commission in Royston, Glasgow for
The Centre. 2002 sees a solo exhibition
at the Fruitmarket Gallery, Edinburgh.
He lives and works in Edinburgh, where
he teaches sculpture at Edinburgh
College of Art.

Paul Carter makes works from the position of an
agnostic. He has made a series of works that attempt,
in a light-hearted way, to seek answers to fundamental
questions of religious belief. Carter has created a series
of mobile structures and improvised shelters that both
broadcast to, and attempt to record a response from
imagined heavens.

The Heaven Search Station, 2001, is a re-working of
an earlier work first shown in 1998 and subsequently
seen throughout Scotland with the Travelling Gallery in
2000. A neon sign reading 'speak to me', designed to
be read from above, is mounted on a trailer. Beneath it
is a radio transmitter and receiver. The transmitter
emits the repeated phrase 'heaven holds a place for',
whilst the radio receiver awaits a response. The phrase
is taken from Simon and Garfunkel's song *Mrs
Robinson*, 1968. Carter adopted the lyric after a copy of
their Greatest Hits that he purchased from a charity
shop stuck on this song. The half-line is repeated
continuously so that it resembles a mantra demanding
an answer to the question of for whom heaven holds a
place. In this way it recalls the incomplete and ambiguous expression 'Et in Arcadia Ego' (and in Arcadia I)
coined by Virgil and popularised in the seventeenth
century by the painter Nicholas Poussin. RT

REFERENCE

East of Eden, Travelling Gallery,
Edinburgh, 2000

The Heaven Search Station 2000
neon sign, recording and transmitting equipment · courtesy the artist

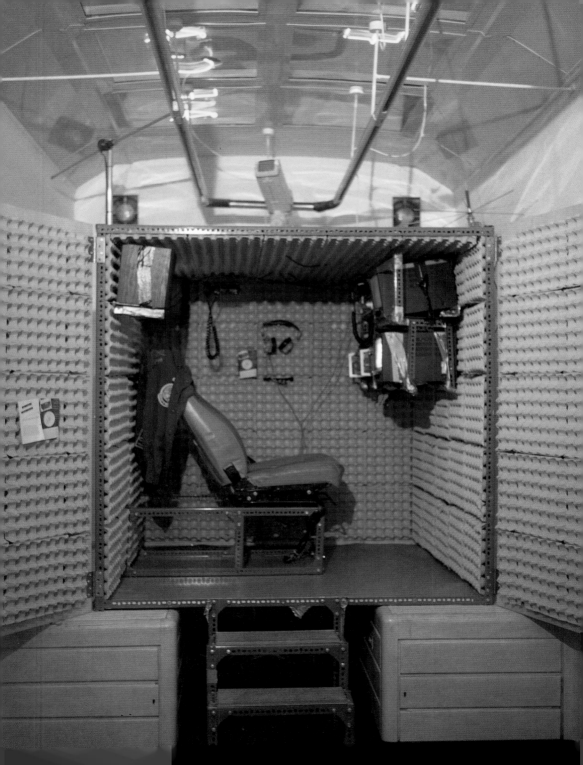

Nathan **Coley**

Born in Glasgow in 1967, Nathan Coley studied in the Environmental Art Department at Glasgow School of Art graduating in 1989. His first solo exhibition was at the Crawford Arts Centre, St Andrews in 1992. He has participated in several significant group exhibitions involving artists from Scotland including *Windfall '91*, Glasgow in 1991 (which he co-organised), *New Art in Scotland*, CCA, Glasgow in 1994 and Aberdeen Art Gallery in 1995, *Sawn-Off*, Stockholm, in 1996, *Glasgow Kunsthalle Bern*, in 1997, *Correspondences* at the Landesmuseum für Moderne Kunst, Berlin in 1997 and at the Scottish National Gallery of Modern Art in 1998 and *Nettverk – Glasgow*, the Museum of Contemporary Art, Oslo in 1998. In 2001 he was the recipient of a Scottish Arts Council Creative Scotland Award and the Henry Moore Sculpture Fellowship at Duncan of Jordanstone College of Art, Dundee. Coley has exhibited extensively across Europe. He lives and works in Dundee.

REFERENCES

Fourteen Churches of Münster, Westfälischer Kunstverein, Münster, 2000

Nathan Coley – A Public Announcement, The Changing Room, Stirling, 1999

Urban Sanctuary, Stills, Edinburgh, 1997

Nathan Coley's work is concerned with revealing the unwritten codes of convention that surround physical structures. A series of slide projections and videos, with accompanying commentary, examine buildings as diverse as the Belém Tower in Lisbon, a world heritage site, to public park shelters in Berlin.

Urban Sanctuary, 1997, was a public artwork commissioned by Stills, Edinburgh during their redevelopment. The commission demanded that the work refer to the building or the processes that were employed in the development. Accordingly Coley chose to make a study of the creation of space pursuing the notion of sanctuary. The work takes the form of a book in which Coley transcribes a series of discussions on the theme he made with individuals that included an architect, an artist, a theologian, a Feng Shui consultant and a policeman.

Fourteen Churches of Münster, 2000, consists of video documentation of Coley's circumnavigation by helicopter of the churches of this German city. The flight recreates an imagined path taken by allied bombers over the city during the Second World War when churches were specifically targeted in order to demoralise civilian populations. Coley's interest was in the way that religious buildings, as architectural constructions, still hold great significance to our cultural identity even though their spiritual significance has declined. **RT**

Fourteen Churches of Münster 2000
video still and flight map · courtesy the artist

Alan **Currall**

Born in 1964 in Stoke-on-Trent, Alan Currall studied at Staffordshire University before going to Glasgow to undertake the MA in Fine Art in 1993–95. He was included in *New Art in Scotland* at CCA, Glasgow in 1994 and Aberdeen Art Gallery in 1995 and *New Contemporaries* in 1996 at Tate Liverpool and Camden Arts Centre, London. His work has been included in numerous group exhibitions throughout the UK and abroad. In 1998 he was the recipient of the Richard Hough Bursary for photography and in 2001 he was selected for the Scottish Arts Council's residency in Canberra. His most recent project *Encyclop3/4dia and Other Works* has been shown in Stoke-on-Trent, Edinburgh and Melbourne.

Alan Currall's work takes the form of straight, documentary-style videos which explore the transference of knowledge, often in quite humorous scenarios. *Word Processor* shows a micro-chip, to which instructions are given by the voice of someone absent from the screen but for a hand. The hand gesticulates and points as if to emphasise what is being said. But the mute, immobile micro-chip is, of course, impervious to the lengthy, detailed instructions, which describe the sequence of events necessary to translate the pressing of a key on a keyboard to the performance of the required action. This piece shares with Currall's other works a concern for the subtleties and complexities of meaning and how it is communicated alongside a consideration of the ways in which technological innovation both supports and influences the sharing of knowledge.

For his most recent work, Currall asked friends and family to recount, in an authoritative tone of voice, what they know about a given subject, which was to be part of his *Encyclop3/4dia*. The work looks at how the human brain stores, retrieves and makes use of information. **KB**

REFERENCE

Encylclop3/4dia and Other Works
(CD-rom and book), Film and Video
Umbrella, London, 2000

Word Processor 1993
video still · courtesy the artist

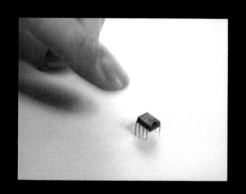

Matthew **Dalziel** + Louise **Scullion**

Born in Irvine in 1957, Matthew Dalziel studied at Duncan of Jordanstone College of Art and Design, Dundee and on the post-graduate course in Sculpture and Fine Art Photography at Glasgow School of Art, which he completed in 1988. Louise Scullion was born in Helensburgh in 1966 and studied at Glasgow School of Art where she graduated from the Environmental Art Department in 1988. Both artists participated independently in the *British Art Show 3* in 1990 and have been working collaboratively since 1992. They have exhibited extensively across Britain and have produced several major public art commissions. In 1995 they participated in *General Release, Young British Artists* at the Venice Biennale, in 1996 they had a joint exhibition at the CCA, Glasgow and in 1997 they exhibited at the Scottish National Gallery of Modern Art, Edinburgh. After several years based in St Combs they are currently living, and working as Research Fellows at Duncan of Jordanstone College of Art, in Dundee.

Dalziel + Scullion's practice gathers their shared interests in landscape, surveillance and new industries. Dalziel was influenced by the impact of petroleum industries on the east coast of Scotland and Scullion by activity in the west by the Ministry of Defence in Loch Long, close to her family home in Helensburgh. Their work in film, video and sculpture offers a highly romanticised vision of the contemporary Scottish landscape. Much of their work from the past decade was made in St Combs, Aberdeenshire, a former fishing village that is now surrounded by defence industries and oil installations.

The Bathers, 1993, was first exhibited at the Institut Français d'Écosse in Edinburgh as part of the *Fotofeis* International Photographic exhibition. The work was the first piece that Dalziel + Scullion made collaboratively and comprises studies of separate individuals set against the evocative landscape in which they then lived. **RT**

'… projects and installations by Dalziel + Scullion seek to set up a space for experiencing art which, while acknowledging the surface texture and sophistication of the modern world, offers in return a quasi-religious and restrained sanctuary in which to reflect and rest from that world.'
Andrew Patrizio, *Contemporary Sculpture in Scotland*, 1999

The Bathers 1993
3 DVD projections onto glass cubicles · courtesy the artists

Jacqueline **Donachie**

Jacqueline Donachie was born in Glasgow in 1969. After studying in the Environmental Art Department of Glasgow School of Art, from which she graduated in 1991, she became a committee member of Transmission Gallery. Her first solo exhibition was the installation *Part Edit* at Tramway in 1994. In 1995–96 she undertook a Fulbright Fellowship on the masters course at Hunter College in New York. She participated in the exhibition *Sawn Off* in Stockholm in 1996 and *Correspondences* at the Scottish National Gallery of Modern Art, Edinburgh and the Martin Gropius Bau, Berlin in 1997. Recent exhibitions have been at the Jerwood Gallery, London (1999) and Spike Island, Bristol (2001), where she was the Henry Moore Fellow. Donachie lives and works in Glasgow.

In both live events and installations, Donachie continues to be fascinated by both the construction and communication of individual identity. Her works have focussed on the ways in which we choose to express our identities, with the social interactions we conceive of on which our sense of self is founded. Several projects, including a clutch of small artist's books, focus on informal story-telling, the use of anecdotes and reminiscences to enable others to construe a sense of who we are or at least of the characters as whom we portray ourselves.

Donachie has frequently used music, both in its role as a vehicle for individual expression and as a social, collective activity. Music first played a significant role in her work with the installation at Tramway, entitled *Part Edit*. The piece comprised four separate audio 'tracks' each including both music and spoken narrative and each played back through a series of bare, exposed speakers mounted in clusters on the walls. The piece is effectively the soundtrack of a life, though whether factual or fictitious is not explicit. Exploiting the power of music to bring about immediate recollection of people, places and events, the piece performs a direct interraction with the viewer's own life experiences. *Part Edit* probes the subjectivity and partiality of memory and the extent to which significance is inferred subsequently in events. Donachie's works continue to explore the ways in which such elements of our cultural lives contribute to the existence of our social being and the ways in which those beings are understood by society. KB

Part Edit 1994
audio installation · courtesy the artist

Chris **Evans**

Born in 1967, Chris Evans studied graphic design at Leicester Polytechnic and on the postgraduate course in Fine Art at Winchester School of Art in Barcelona, completed in 1993. He has lived and worked in Glasgow since 1995. In the same year, together with Duncan Hamilton, he founded the artists-run Three Month Gallery in Liverpool. The two continue to initiate artist's projects as All Horizons Club. In 1998 Evans and Hamilton organised a series of exhibitions in Benefit Agencies across northern England as part of *Artranspennine '98*. Since 1997, together with Caroline Woodley, he has produced *STOPSTOP*, an occasional compendium of artwork by locally based and international artists. Evans has exhibited extensively in Britain and in 1999 completed an artist's research fellowship at the Henry Moore Institute in Leeds.

Chris Evans' practice is characterised by an ambiguous purpose; often mischievous, largely anonymous and frequently subcontracted to peers. In 1999 Evans executed a poster campaign in Kilsyth advertising the reunion of an organisation that doesn't exist; *The Friends of the Divided Mind.*

For *Gemini Sculpture Park*, 2000, Evans established a temporary arts organisation: the UK Corporate Sculpture Consultancy. Under this guise Evans conducted a series of interviews with the directors of companies based in a business park outside Leeds. He asked each of them what they would want from a public sculpture installed in front of their business premises. From these conversations Evans drafted a series of stylised designs and then invited fellow artists (Graham Fagen, Toby Paterson and Padraig Timoney) to create maquettes of proposed artworks and 'artist's impressions' of the site. The work was first exhibited at the Henry Moore Institute in 2000. RT

REFERENCE

Gemini Sculpture Park, UK Sculpture Corporate Sculpture Consultancy, Chris Evans, Henry Moore Institute, Leeds, 2001

Gemini Sculpture Park 2000
silk screen prints, explanatory texts, bronze cast by Graham Fagan, wall drawing by Toby Paterson and oil painting by Padraig Timoney · courtesy the artists and Leeds Museums and Galleries (Leeds City Art Gallery)

Graham **Fagen**

Born in Glasgow in 1966, Graham Fagen studied Sculpture at Glasgow School of Art before undertaking an MA in Art and Architecture at Kent Institute of Art & Design, Canterbury in 1989–90. He subsequently lived in Birmingham, where he worked at Birmingham Institute of Art until 1995 when he returned to Glasgow where he now lives. He has been a lecturer at Duncan of Jordanstone College of Art in Dundee since 1995. In 1998 Fagen had his first solo show at Matt's Gallery, London and in 1999 an exhibition of work was shown at Inverleith House, Royal Botanic Gardens, Edinburgh. He was included in the *British Art Show 5* in 2000 and has taken part in numerous group exhibitions internationally. In 1999–2000 he was chosen for the commission to Kosovo by the Imperial War Museum, London where his subsequent installation, *Theatre* was first shown in 2000.

Graham Fagen's work frequently uses photography and video, often accompanied by text, both spoken and written. The forms his work has taken have tended to suggest the documentary, conveying his interest in how facts are recorded and interpreted in later analyses. In these works, the veracity or otherwise of the objects, scenarios and incidents is never pronounced but left ambiguous. His works have often focussed on marginal communities, such as his installation *Nothank*, 1999, which presents a documentary about a (fictional) peripheral housing scheme through the eyes of all of those involved in its conception, realisation and ongoing use. The *Weapons* series of 1998 depicted home-made weapons, accompanied by descriptions of their making and their application.

Theatre, 2000, is an installation comprising a video projection of a stage play and a selection of objects, some of which appear in the setting for the play. The characters in the play alternate between English and an unidentified foreign language, rendering their speech incomprehensible, though their physical behaviour continues to convey something of their meaning. The action shifts from polite greeting and exchange to bitter dispute and physical aggression, while the inability to understand, through the shifts in language, forces an awareness of our differing responses to conflict. Raising difficult issues to do with objectivity and neutrality in the face of provocation, *Theatre* also looks at the portrayal of the truth and how it is staged. **KB**

REFERENCE

Peek-a-Jobby, Matt's Gallery, London, 1998

Theatre 2000
DVD projection, benches, rubber matting · courtesy the artist, Matt's Gallery and the Imperial War Museum

Keith **Farquhar**

Born in Edinburgh in 1969, Farquhar studied Sculpture at Edinburgh College of Art and at Goldsmiths College, London, where he completed his MA in 1996. He has subsequently participated in many group exhibitions in Britain and abroad. In 2000, together with Lucy McKenzie he established 'Flourish', which provides artists' studios and hosts events, and 'Charisma', which organises exhibitions that have included an exhibition at Transmission Gallery in 2000. He now lives and works in Edinburgh where he works together with patients at the Royal Edinburgh Psychiatric Hospital and teaches in the Sculpture Department at Edinburgh College of Art.

Keith Farquhar's paintings and sculptural installations draw from an eclectic array of sources, from fine art painting tradition and diverse popular culture. His irreverent and humorous work forms a highly personalised and idiosyncratic vocabulary that has recently referred to his relationship with his family, shop window displays, Scottish national identity and Heart of Midlothian Football Club.

At Goldsmiths College, under the tutelage of Michael Craig Martin, Farquhar was persuaded to take up painting. He subsequently established his reputation with a series of paintings that appropriated the illustrations found on sociological textbook covers published in the 1960's and 1970's. Farquhar reproduced some of these designs with marker pens onto canvases primed with white household gloss paint to recall diagrams drawn by lecturers on whiteboards. These paintings, such as *Stigma*, 1997, *The Phenomenology of Moral Experience*, 1996, and *Q. What does woman want? A. What the women want,* 1998, adopt their titles from the books whose cover designs inspired them. The paintings where made in tribute to the ideas of R.D. Laing and are, in some sense, a memorial to the demise of the romantic ideas of the Glasgow-born psychiatrist. **RT**

REFERENCE

Phoenix Specific, Keith Farquhar, Stefan Thater, Kunsthaus Hamburg, 2001

Q. What does woman want?
A. What the women want 1998
acrylic on canvas · courtesy the artist and Anthony Reynolds Gallery

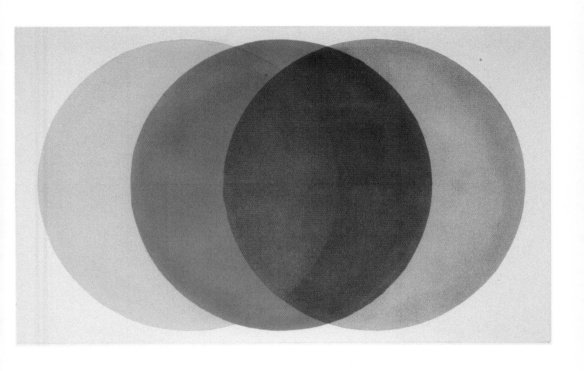

Moyna **Flannigan**

Born in Edinburgh in 1963, Flannigan studied at Edinburgh College of Art and at Yale University School of Art, New York where she completed her studies in 1987. In 1990 she had a solo exhibition at Aberdeen Art Gallery and she has subsequently participated in several group exhibitions in Britain and abroad. She had a solo exhibition at the CCA, Glasgow in 1996 and the following year she was awarded a scholarship to the British School in Rome. She was shortlisted for the NatWest Art Prize in 1999. In 2001 she participated in *Open Country* a survey of contemporary Scottish Art in Lausanne. She lives and works in Edinburgh and teaches at Glasgow School of Art.

Moyna Flannigan's paintings are made without models, the aid of photography or preparatory drawings but are produced spontaneously, directly onto canvas from her memory and experience. Flannigan employs as few brush marks as possible as paint is pushed about the canvas to create casual facial expressions and to form loose folds in the subjects' clothes.

Flannigan's paintings are not portraits but composite images derived from her own imagination. In paintings such as *Just Like Daddy*, her subjects are uncannily familiar. These are individuals whom we may seem to recognise by their clothes or expressions as belonging to a particular social stratum or place. We may also recognise their poses from a society portrait, from art history or an iconic photograph. However, by introducing exaggerated, unnaturalistic colour Flannigan places her paintings firmly in the present. RT

'Colour is not an adjunct, as it were, to the subject matter but is an integral, even prime factor. She builds it up slowly, layer by layer, with the result that the final surface is rich and complex. The figure still remains the armature around which her paintings are built, but it is the process of painting which is as much the subject matter.'
Keith Hartley, *Locale*, City Art Centre Edinburgh, 1999

REFERENCE

Moyna Flannigan, Paintings, CCA, Glasgow, 1996

Just Like Daddy 1998
oil on canvas · courtesy the artist and the Scottish National Gallery of Modern Art

Douglas **Gordon**

Born in Glasgow in 1966, Douglas Gordon studied in the Environmental Art Department at Glasgow School of Art and in 1988–90 undertook an MA at the Slade School of Art, London. He was a committee member at Transmission Gallery, Glasgow from 1990–92 and a co-organiser of the *Windfall* exhibition in Glasgow in 1991. He also participated in the exhibitions *Self-Conscious State* at the Third Eye Centre, Glasgow in 1990 and *Guilt by Association* at the Irish Museum of Modern Art, Dublin in 1992. His first solo exhibition was *24 Hour Psycho* at Tramway, Glasgow in 1993. Since then his work has been included in innumerable group exhibitions throughout the world and he has been the subject of major solo exhibitions at, among others, the Kunstverein Hannover, Musée d'Art moderne de la Ville de Paris, Tate Gallery Liverpool, and, in 2001, the Museum of Contemporary Arts, Los Angeles. Gordon has participated in several of the most important international exhibitions of recent years, including the 1995 and 1999 Venice Biennale exhibitions and *Sculpture Projects, Münster* in 1997. He won the Turner Prize in 1996 and the Hugo Boss Prize in 1998. He lives and works in Glasgow and New York.

REFERENCES

Kidnapped, Van Abbemuseum, Eindhoven, 1998

Douglas Gordon, Kunstverein Hannover, 1998

Douglas Gordon's works often express an opposition, between good and evil, light and dark, right and wrong. Such ambiguity has been explicit in a number of works that use fictional narratives from popular film and literature, such as *The Private Memoirs and Confessions of a Justified Sinner*, 1995/96, a two-screen video projection using footage from a 1930s film of Robert Louis Stevenson's famous tale of Jekyll and Hyde.

In tandem with his well-known video projection works, including *24 Hour Psycho* commissioned by and shown at Tramway in 1993, Gordon has consistently produced a series of text works, exploiting the power of words presented in a specific environment to conjure memories, fears and anxieties from the mind of the viewer. First shown in Sète, France in 1997, *From God to Nothing* is an installation comprising white text on a dark blue wall illuminated only by three bare bulbs, suspended at the height of the head, the heart and the sex. The text lists 150 fears from ' fear of God' to 'fear of nothing', while the lights serve to keep present in the viewer a sense of the seat of those fears. Conjuring memories of horror films and stories or even of more direct, personal incidents, the installation conveys a sense of the psychological self's reactions to experience and knowledge. Such an emphasis on the psychological self is characteristic of Gordon's work, in which it is often weighed against the physically insubstantial. Both video and text-based works share strong sculptural qualities in his use of space and the explicit positioning of the viewer within the work. **KB**

From God to Nothing 1997
installation: 3 light bulbs, wall paint, text · courtesy the artist and FRAC Languedoc-Roussillon

fear of god
fear of devil
fear of jesus
fear of judgement
fear of purgatory
fear of heaven
fear of hell
fear of friends
fear of enemies
fear of failure
fear of success
fear of food
fear of water
fear of blood
fear of own mother
fear of own father
fear of own sister
fear of own brother
fear of own son
fear of own daughter
fear of nakedness
fear of breasts
fear of the vagina
fear of the penis
fear of swollen membrane
fear of sexual intercourse
fear of rape
fear of castration
fear of masturbation
fear of teeth
fear of teeth falling out
fear of oral penetration
fear of the anal penetration
fear of men
fear of women
fear of children
fear of dwarfs
fear of tall people
fear of youth
fear of the elderly
fear of authority
fear of moving objects
fear of broken bones
fear of being crippled
fear of physical pain
fear of disfiguration
fear of surgery
fear of anaesthesia
fear of coma
fear of psychological pain
fear of seizure
fear of being poisoned
fear of dying
fear of dying after parents
fear of dying before parents
fear of living too long
fear of dying too young
fear of everlasting life
fear of the dead
fear of burial
fear of burial, while still alive
fear of cremation
fear of cremation, while still alive
fear of the exhumation
fear of sleep
fear of waking up
fear of falling asleep and never waking up
fear of never being able to sleep again
fear of sleeping alone
fear of loneliness
fear of love
fear of marriage
fear of loss of sense of self
fear of ego
fear of self-hatred
fear of kindness
fear of rejection
fear of tenderness
fear of laughter
fear of crying
fear of blindness
fear of deafness
fear of the inability to express oneself
fear of lying
fear of being lied to
fear of strangers
fear of large crowds of people
fear of public space
fear of moving at high speed
fear of flying
fear of falling
fear of drowning
fear of the sea
fear of fish
fear of birds
fear of dogs
fear of cats
fear of spiders
fear of flying insects
fear of crawling insects
fear of reptiles
fear of the dark
fear of suffocation
fear of gas
fear of electricity
fear of telephones
fear of televisions
fear of knives
fear of smoke
fear of fire
fear of bathing
fear of urination
fear of defecating
fear of bodily functions
fear of uncleanliness
fear of infection
fear of aids
fear of cancer
fear of nature
fear of reality
fear of loss of reality
fear of money
fear of poverty
fear of white
fear of black
fear of fog
fear of thunder
fear of lightening
fear of bright light
fear of bright colour
fear of fame
fear of anonymity
fear of open spaces
fear of enclosure
fear of collapsing building
fear of technology
fear of intellect
fear of the supernatural
fear of fear
fear of inquisition
fear of prophesy
fear of the future
fear of the past
fear of the present
fear of time passing
fear of the end of the world
fear of the truth
fear of knowledge
fear of solipsism
fear of nothing

Kate **Gray**

Born in Edinburgh in 1971, Kate Gray studied Sculpture at Sheffield Hallam University between 1990 and 1993 and on the MA course at Glasgow School of Art between 1994 and 1996. She has exhibited extensively in Scotland and abroad. In 2001 Gray had a further solo exhibition at the Collective Gallery. She lives and works in Edinburgh.

Kate Gray creates images of apocalyptic landscapes populated by futuristic, prototypical figures. These have been presented as still photographs or as video sculpture. Gray utilises existing images, such as photojournalism of natural disasters, that she combines with her own footage, photographed or digitally created. In doing so she aims to destabilise the images as a series of records of actual events to create work that hovers between science fiction and reality.

Raft, 1999, consists of a video projection of a struggling, androgynous computer generated figure projected onto a squirming surface of Styrofoam pellets in a cardboard box. Gray's computer generated character is seen to struggle in a vortex of packaging material. Film, and digital manipulation, of which *Raft* is an example, have meant that seeing and believing have become increasingly disconnected in our minds. Gray's work is concerned with this doubt. **RT**

REFERENCES

The Ghost of a Flea, The Collective Gallery, Edinburgh, 2001

East of Eden, Travelling Gallery, Edinburgh, 2000

Raft 1999
DVD projection, styrofoam, motor and cardboard box · courtesy the artist

Kevin **Henderson**

Born in Singapore in 1963, Kevin Henderson studied at Gray's School of Art in Aberdeen. He participated in a number of important group exhibitions including *Scatter* at the Third Eye Centre, Glasgow (1989), *The British Art Show 3* (1990), *Self-Conscious State* at the Third Eye Centre, Glasgow (1990) and *Guilt by Association* (1992) at the Irish Museum of Modern Art in Dublin. Based in Dundee, Henderson's work is now multi-disciplinary, involving music, performance and writing. He is Course Director of the MFA at Duncan of Jordanstone College of Art & Design in Dundee.

Originally working as a painter, Henderson began to work with objects in the early 1990s, combining them with painted signs and symbols derived from a diverse range of original sources. The past is inscribed in the objects used by Kevin Henderson, their previous uses and abuses somehow apparent or suggested in their surfaces. **KB**

'I like to feel that I can work with any material. I'm not biased towards any one thing but if I moved from where I am living now, then the materials I use would undoubtedly change … Ideas or concepts, regardless of importance, are similarly only materials. They are there to be used – like images, of the things the works are assembled from, they are intrinsic to the construction of meaning.'
Kevin Henderson in *British Art Show 3*, 1990

Untitled 1990
found object, indian ink · courtesy the artist

Annette **Heyer**

Born in Hamburg in 1960, Annette Heyer has lived and worked in Scotland since 1986. She is currently based in Linlithgow. Heyer has taught in the Photography and Painting Departments of Glasgow School of Art since 1991 and also teaches at Chelsea School of Art, London. In recent years, she has had solo exhibitions at Street Level Gallery in Glasgow and Angel Row in Nottingham. In 2000 the Fruitmarket Gallery, Edinburgh presented a solo exhibition of Heyer's recent work, entitled – *As for the future,* as part of its 'Visions for the Future' project.

Annette Heyer's work incorporates both photography and objects. Her works have consistently conveyed an interest in the physicality of light and the notion of temporality, of moments between others. Her photographic works of the early 1990s such as *Bounded Waters*, 1992, are deeply ambiguous images, whose resonance lies in the intense contrast between dark and light, provoking a consideration of the very essence of photography and its material basis. These images – of sheets of glass immersed in water – highlight the fact of the image as a two-dimensional surface. While the interplay between dark and light inevitably triggers attempts to read what appears before us as something other than surface, the resultant understanding leads only to an absent surface. What we see in the areas of light is in fact neither the glass nor the water but the tiny pockets of air that adhere to the glass surface as it is immersed.

Her more recent work *Lightbox*, 2000, captures the shadow cast by a plant now entirely absent both from the gallery space and the image. It now appears only by means of the merest trace of light cast on a membrane-like surface. What we are left with is a play of absence and presence, light and dark. **KB**

REFERENCE

As for the future, Fruitmarket Gallery, Edinburgh, 2001

Bounded Waters 1992
black and white photographs · courtesy the artist

Steve **Hollingsworth**

Born in Leeds in 1967, Steve Hollingsworth studied at Gwent College of Higher Education and on the MFA course at Glasgow School of Art between 1992 and 1994. His first solo exhibitions were in 2000 at the Fruitmarket Gallery, Edinburgh and the Turnpike Gallery, Leigh. He has exhibited extensively in Scotland participating in *New Art in Scotland*, CCA, Glasgow in 1994. In 1998 and 1999 Hollingsworth participated on the Research Programme at the CCA Kitakyushu, Japan and in 2001 he began a further residency at Grizedale in the Lake District. He lives and works in Glasgow and teaches at the University of Northumbria, Newcastle.

Like several of his peers Steve Hollingsworth utilises furniture in his sculptural practice. With the addition of neon and argon lights and refrigeration units salvaged from domestic fridges, Hollingsworth imbues these everyday objects with a transcendent quality.

Ice Chair utilises a tubular steel and canvas chair found by Hollingsworth under which he installed a fridge mechanism that causes thick ice to form on the chair's metal frame. *Electric Chair* is a tubular glass replica of the metal frame of *Ice Chair*. This glass vessel is filled with charged argon that illuminates the structure – its cold blue aura echoes the ice coating of its pair. Both works involve objects that are transformed by the use of gasses. RT

REFERENCE

Steve Hollingsworth, Fruitmarket Gallery, Edinburgh, 2000

Ice Chair 1996
chair, refrigeration unit · courtesy the artist

Louise **Hopkins**

Born in 1965 in Hertfordshire, England, Hopkins studied at Newcastle-upon-Tyne Polytechnic. From 1992–94 she undertook an MA at Glasgow School of Art, since when she has continued to live in Glasgow. Her first solo exhibition was at Ben Grady Gallery in Canberra, Australia. In 1994 she participated in the *New Art in Scotland* exhibition at the CCA, Glasgow and had her first solo show in the UK at Aberdeen Art Gallery. In 1996 she was included in the *New Contemporaries* exhibition at Tate Liverpool and Camden Arts Centre, London. Hopkins' work has been included in numerous group exhibitions internationally, including *Glasgow* at the Kunsthalle Bern in 1997, *Prime*, Dundee Contemporary Arts' inaugural exhibition in 1999 and *Open Country* at the Musée Cantonal des Beaux-Arts de Lausanne in 2001. Hopkins lives in Glasgow.

Domestic furnishing fabric has been the literal and conceptual basis of much of Louise Hopkins' work. What Hopkins does to the fabric is to re-cover its particularity, to rediscover the original marks, which at some point in the distant past constituted the designs with which she works. The printed marks that appear on the fabric have been derived from a now anonymous designer's drawings. Hopkins' brush strokes emulate and accompany the printed marks, surrounding but not covering them, almost re-animating them. The printed imagery becomes just one selection of marks from thousands of possibilities.

These works on fabric are accompanied by a series of paintings on various forms of printed paper, notably song sheets and maps. Like the fabric works, they force the viewer to re-consider the original marks, symbols, and demarcations that make up the document. Collapsing time and space, they connect us with the labour of their original making. They have an even stronger sense of stifling claustrophobia or at least constraint, eliminating as they do the possibility for the printed matter to do what it ought, and guide us to something or somewhere else. From something legible, familiar and essentially functional emerges a strange and disturbing new image, an alternative truth through a direct connection with the absent mark-maker. **KB**

REFERENCE
Louise Hopkins, Tramway, Glasgow / Andrew Mummery Gallery, London, 1996

Europe Map (land) (1) 1998
acrylic ink on map · courtesy the artist and the Scottish National Gallery of Modern Art

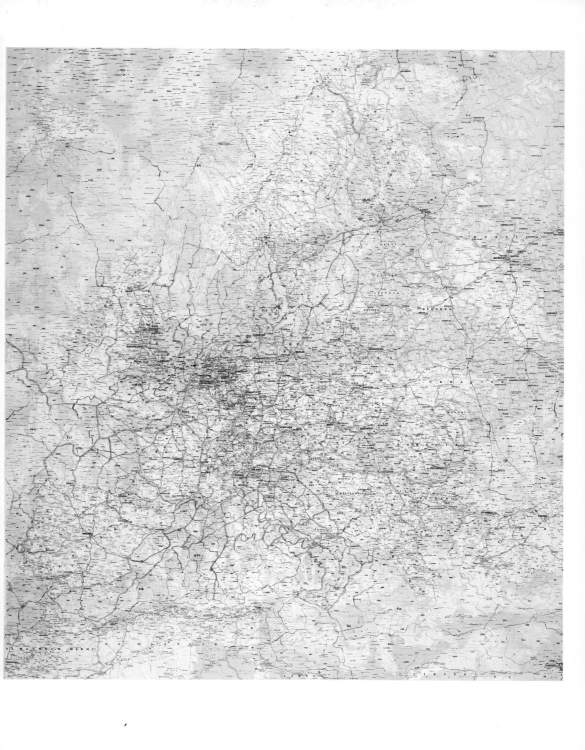

Kenny **Hunter**

Born in Edinburgh in 1962, Kenny Hunter studied Sculpture at Glasgow School of Art between 1983 and 1987. He had his first solo exhibition at the Norwich Gallery in 1996. He has exhibited extensively in Britain and abroad with solo exhibitions at Arnolfini, Bristol, in 1998, Leeds Metropolitan University Gallery, in 1998 and in 1999 the Scottish National Portrait Gallery, Edinburgh. In 2000 he exhibited at Glasgow Print Studio. Hunter has created a number of high profile, commissioned works in Scotland including; *Cherub/ Skull*, 1997, for the Tron Theatre, Glasgow, *Man walks among us*, 2000, for Glasgow Museums, and *Citizen Fire Fighter*, 2001, outside Glasgow's Central Station. Hunter lives and works in Glasgow.

Hunter's sculptural practice offers a contemporary take on traditional figurative sculpture; referencing Classical and Biblical themes and those of portraiture. Hunter often inserts contemporary political ideas that run counter to these traditions of remembrance, triumphalism or pride. A pair of bookend busts *What is History?*, 2000, offers two fleeting figures from our recent history: Monica Lewinsky, who had a brief sexual relationship with the then President of the United States, and Osama Bin Laden, a 'terrorist' who is said to have been demonised by the same American administration to divert media attention from the controversy that resulted from the President's affair.

Bad Conscience and the Old Skool Plastik, 2000, is most indicative of Hunter's recent practice and his position as a maker of contemporary monuments. The 'Bad conscience' of the title refers to the collective guilt we may have for the many examples of public sculpture that celebrate colonial conflict; 'the Old Skool Plastik' to his affection for the plastic arts. The work parodies public works as it portrays a 'pile' (the noun of choice for cynical sculptural criticism) of money, skulls and bones, and dispensed gun cartridges. The work bears the inscription 'Finis Gloria Mundi' (end of worldly glory). RT

REFERENCES

Kenny Hunter, Invisible Republic, Glasgow Print Studio, Glasgow 2000

Kenny Hunter, Work 1995–1998, Arnolfini, Bristol, 1998

Bad Conscience and the Old Skool Plastik 2000
glass-reinforced plastic, paint · courtesy the artist

Callum **Innes**

Born in Edinburgh in 1962, Callum Innes studied at Gray's School of Art in Aberdeen before undertaking a post-graduate course at Edinburgh College of Art from 1984–85. He participated in the exhibitions *Scatter* at the Third Eye Centre, Glasgow in 1989 and *The British Art Show 3* in 1990. He had his first solo show at Frith Street Gallery, London in 1990 and the following year solo shows were presented at the ICA, London and the Scottish National Gallery of Modern Art in Edinburgh. Since then Innes' work has been exhibited extensively in Europe and the U.S. He was short-listed for the Turner Prize in 1995 and was awarded the Nat West Art Prize in 1998. In 1999 solo shows of Innes' work were held at the Ikon Gallery, Birmingham, the Irish Museum of Modern Art, Dublin and the Kunsthalle, Bern. Innes lives in Edinburgh and is a research fellow at Glasgow School of Art.

Throughout the 1990s Callum Innes' paintings have consistently explored the ability of paint to capture an event. His works are very much the result of actions, the outcome of incident. Rather than building up layers of paint on to a prepared surface, Innes' way of working is more accurately described as 'depainting', as the specific detail of the final work is dependent on an action of removal or erasure rather than addition or application. The series of works from the early 1990s collectively referred to as the *Identified Forms* show the impact of turpentine on the immaculately painted surfaces of solid colour, the 'forms' referred to in the title being absences rather than presences. The outlines and eventual shapes of these forms are dictated simply by time – the time taken for the turpentine to move across the surface before it (quickly) evaporates, having stripped away the paint in its path.

The interplay between presence and absence has developed through Innes' more recent series of *Exposed Paintings*, in which a broad band of colour is applied through a section of the prepared canvas, only to have a substantial part of it removed, to varying degrees, by the application of turpentine. The remaining marks bear traces of movement and of the constituent elements of the now absent colour, indicating the painting's past. **KB**

'Each individual painting has the particularity and personality of a cherished family photo, a fact under-scored rather than undermined by occasional, inevitable family resemblances. Like a photograph, a painting by Callum Innes is a moment arrested in time.'
Caoimhín Mac Giolla Léith in *Callum Innes*, Ikon Gallery, 1998

REFERENCES

Callum Innes (1990–96), Inverleith House, The Royal Botanic Garden, Edinburgh, 1996

Callum Innes, Ikon Gallery, Birmingham / Kunsthalle Bern, 1998

82

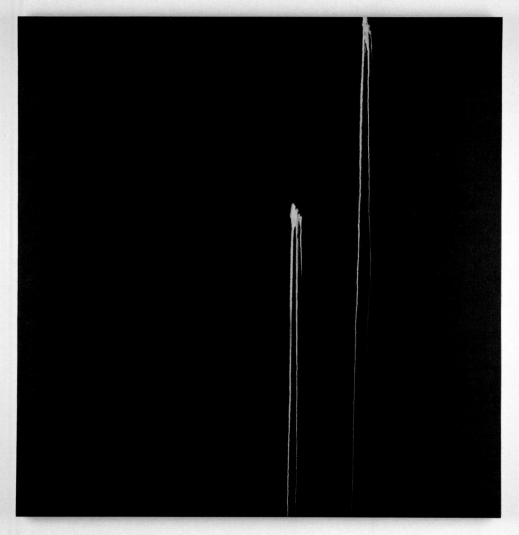

Two Identified Forms 1995
oil on canvas · private collection

Iain **Kettles** and Susie **Hunter**

Born in Glasgow in 1966, Iain Kettles studied Environmental Art at Glasgow School of Art, graduating in 1989. He participated in *Windfall '91*, Glasgow and had his first solo exhibition at Transmission Gallery in 1992. Susie Hunter was born in Dumfries in 1967 and studied Silversmithing and Jewellery at Glasgow School of Art, graduating in 1990. Kettles and Hunter have been working collaboratively since 1993. Their first joint exhibition was in 1993 at Intermedia, Glasgow. In 2001 they had exhibitions at Kunsthallen Brandts Klædefabrik, Odense and at Nikolaj, Copenhagen. Kettles and Hunter live and work in Glasgow.

Kettles and Hunter's collaborative work comprises large inflatable sculptures fashioned from brightly coloured nylon. Their work has been compared to cinematic moments where animated characters escape from two dimensionality to appear in the physical world. The flat-coloured fabric of their works lies in sharp contrast to the rough surroundings of the former industrial spaces in which their work is often presented. Similarly the physical scale of their works often appears to defy the light material from which they are made.

Inflatable Ladder, 1996, is a vastly oversized, silver, inflatable ladder that was first exhibited in the Old Fruitmarket, Glasgow. The work was included as part of *Girls' High*, 1996, an exhibition to celebrate ten years of Glasgow School of Art's Environmental Art Department. *It's a Girl*, 1998, is a nylon inflatable pink rabbit; an oversized facsimile of a child's metallic helium balloon. The work was first exhibited as part of 'Host' at Tramway, Glasgow in 1998. RT

'Kettles and Hunter's inflatable works are fleeting, transient, made from air, nothing really. Because they never have any discernible function they are free to simple *glow*, roaming the hazy outlines of the imagination.'
Ross Sinclair, 'Storing up the static, the inflatable art of Kettles and Hunter', *Space Invader*

REFERENCES

Space Invader, Tramway, Glasgow, 1999

It's a Girl 1998
nylon, electric fan · courtesy the artists

Jim **Lambie**

Born in Glasgow in 1964, Lambie worked in the music industry before studying at Glasgow School of Art, graduating in 1994. He had his first solo exhibition at Transmission Gallery in 1999 and has subsequently participated in group exhibitions in major public galleries including Kunsthalle Basel and The Moderna Museet, Stockholm. In 2000 Lambie participated in the *British Art Show 5*, and in *Dream Machines* at Dundee Contemporary Arts and Camden Arts Centre, London. In the same year he was awarded the Paul Hamlyn Foundation award to Artists. In 2001 Lambie participated in *Painting at the Edge of the World* at the Walker Art Center, Minneapolis. He is currently based in New York.

Jim Lambie is best known for his large-scale floor installation *ZOBOP*, 1999, which consists of hundreds of concentric strips of coloured vinyl tape that he applies to gallery floors. The work echoes architectural features of its surroundings whilst, at the same time appears as a vortex, referring to other, less tangible, dimensions.

Fascinated by the way in which music can transform a social environment Lambie has created a number of works that that utilise record decks adorned with glitter and ephemeral objects such as coat hangers, belts, plastic tape and safety pins. Such works as *Handbag*, *Garage* and *Graffiti*, all 2000, transform now obsolete technology into fetishistic artefacts.

Lambie's signature work is an ongoing series of *Psychedelic Soul Sticks* that consist of bamboo canes and other unspecified objects that are wrapped in reams of brightly coloured thread. Lambie's shamanic artworks appear to transcend physical space and induce reverie. **RT**

REFERENCE

ZOBOP, Transmission Gallery, Glasgow / The Showroom, London, 2001

Graffiti 1999
turntable, glitter, safety pins, plastic · courtesy the artist and The Modern Institute

Tracy **Mackenna** and Edwin **Janssen**

Born in Oban in 1963, Tracy Mackenna studied at Glasgow School of Art where she completed her studies in 1986. Her first solo exhibition was at the Graeme Murray Gallery in Edinburgh in 1990. She subsequently had solo exhibitions at the CCA, Glasgow, and the Arnolfini Gallery, Bristol, in 1993. Since 1997 she has worked collaboratively with Edwin Janssen (born Amstelveen, 1961) with whom she has participated in several international exhibitions, including Manifesta in Rotterdam in 1996, *Artranspennine '98*, *Peace* at the Migros Museum, Zürich in 1999 and *As It Is* at the Ikon Gallery, Birmingham in 2000. Recent projects have included *Soft* at the Pier Arts Centre, Stromness, 2000, and *Ed and Ellis in Ever Ever Land*, CCA, Glasgow, 2001. Mackenna lives and works in Glasgow and Rotterdam and teaches at Duncan of Jordanstone College of Art and Design in Dundee.

Mackenna and Janssen's collaborative work often entails long periods spent working in the galleries in which they are invited to exhibit. They work directly with the thoughts, ideas and attitudes of the visitors they encounter, frequently rendering their interactions in the form of wool blankets, a material imbued with associations of domesticity, privacy and protection. These works come to form an unusual portrait of a particular time and place, and of the people who inhabit it.

The *Peace Blanket* was made during an exhibition at the Migros Museum in Zürich in 1999. It is comprised of comments made to Mackenna and Janssen by visitors to the exhibition, asked about what the idea of peace meant to them now. The selected phrases were rendered in felt, then tacked onto the white blanket. On the last day of the exhibition, it was sent back to Scotland to be machine finished, reducing all the accumulated layers into one integrated layer. The blanket is accompanied by a photograph of Mackenna and Janssen re-enacting John Lennon and Yoko Ono's famous 'Bed In' at the time of their marriage in 1969 and a remake of their 'War is Over' poster. The project as a whole asks us to re-examine our thoughts about peace and how they may have changed from those of a different time. KB

Peace Blanket 1999–2000
wool, felt, silk · courtesy the artists and the Migros Museum, Zürich

FIGHTING FOR FREEDOM
IS LIKE

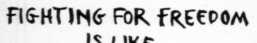
Kareen and Urs are not peacely mooded at the moment

FUCKING FOR VIRGINITY

a state of quiet   PEACE   light blue
                          AND
stillness   LOVE   KEINER LIEBT MICH

NIE   konnten selber nicht freundlich ge
WIEDER   Die wir den Boden bereiten, wollten zu

It's easier to think about peace in summer than during bittercold Novemberdays

As if remembering something from the distant past

freedom from disturbance

          MAKE   Erasmus is born
          LOVE
MAN SOLLTE NICHT FINDEN, WAS MAN SUCHT

GLÜCK GLÜCK GLÜCK JE   WAR   TON STÜCK

cessation of war   WE HAD
                                                GET REAL
WAR   tranquility
IS OVER!   peace of mind   A DREAM

                              I don't have anything meaningful to say

IF YOU WANT IT   freedom from contention

Chad **McCail**

Born in Manchester in 1961, McCail studied English at the Universiy of Kent before studying Fine Art at Goldsmiths College, London, graduating in 1989. He had his first solo exhibition at the Collective Gallery, Edinburgh in 1998 and has subsequently participated in many group exhibitions internationally including the Melbourne Biennial in 1999. In 2000 McCail participated in the *British Art Show 5* and in the same year he was shortlisted for the inaugural Beck's Futures Prize. Chad McCail lives and works in Edinburgh.

Chad McCail is best known for paintings and drawings that parody children's books, appearing as a series of didactic guides for making the world a better place. In McCail's utopia 'prisoners are freed', 'money is destroyed', 'soldiers leave the armed forces', 'people stop using things', 'take turns to do the difficult jobs' and 'have relaxing orgasms'. The works are informed by, amongst others, the writings of the psychologist Wilhelm Reich (1897–1957) an associate of Sigmund Freud who 'discovered' the life energy that he termed 'orgone'.

Whilst recent works by McCail present plans for a utopia, earlier works such as *Aerial*, 1996, and *Spring*, 1997, depict dystopia as city suburbs descend into chaos. The drawings resemble architects' or town planners' maps. Such cold, inexpressive models are transformed by McCail by the introduction of violence. In McCail's town an insurrection appears to be taking place; a train is being looted, razor wire is being erected around the school, a road bridge has collapsed, police vehicles are ablaze and the military have arrived. RT

Spring 1997
pencil on paper · courtesy the artist, Laurent Delaye and the British Council

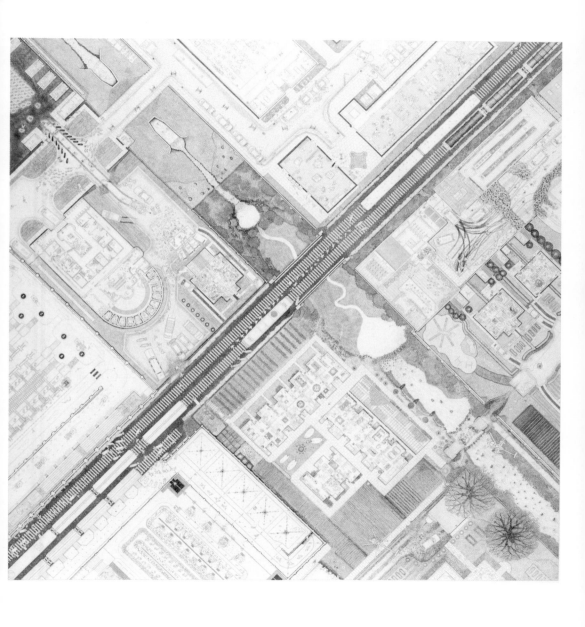

Lucy **McKenzie**

Born in Glasgow in 1977, McKenzie studied Painting at Duncan of Jordanstone College of Art and Design in Dundee, graduating in 1999. After exhibiting at the Cabinet Gallery, London in 2000 she had her first major exhibition at Inverleith House, Edinburgh. In 1999, together with other artists she established 'Flourish' which provides artists' studios and hosts events. In 2000 McKenzie participated in the *British Art Show 5* and she was shortlisted for the inaugural Beck's Futures Prize. In 2001 she participated in a major international painting exhibition, *Painting at the Edge of the World* at the Walker Art Center, Minneapolis. She lives and works in Glasgow.

Lucy McKenzie's paintings are filled with an eclectic mixture of signs and symbols of the twentieth century including images from the Olympic games, of designs by Charles Rennie Mackintosh and logos of the disbanded Strathclyde regional authority. McKenzie reconfigures such eclectic icons of design and history to create an idiosyncratic discourse between the different ideologies and fashions that they represent.

Subventionieren, 2000, incorporates a typical combination of Olympic imagery and self portraiture. McKenzie's fascination with Olympic imagery concentrates on the highly politicised games of the early 1980's when the marketing material was used as cold war propaganda.

Force the Hand of Choice, 2000, presents a group of pianists performing at the opening ceremony of the 1984 Summer Games in Los Angeles, the image is abstracted to resemble a Vorticist painting of the 1920's. The painting is a reworking of an earlier watercolour, *Fear of Jazz*, 2000, that was first exhibited at the ICA, London in 2000.

Poised Campbell, 2000, is a painting of a Steven Campbell performance, *Poised Murder*, organised whilst he was a student at Glasgow School of Art in 1981. Campbell's stage set, like McKenzie's paintings holds several reference points to art history including what Campbell described as a 'Vorticist zig-zag floor'. RT

Subventionieren 2000
oil and acrylic on canvas · courtesy the artist and Cabinet Gallery, London

Wendy **McMurdo**

Born in Edinburgh in 1962, Wendy McMurdo initially studied painting. She later studied at the Pratt Institute in New York and completed an MA at Gold-smiths College, London in 1993. She now lives in Edinburgh. Her first solo exhibition *In a Shaded Place – the Digital and the Uncanny* travelled widely throughout the UK and Europe in 1995–96. Her work has been included in a number of group exhibitions interna-tionally, including *Uncanny* at the Fotomuseum, Winterthur in 1999 and *Open Country: Contemporary Scottish Artists* at the Musée Cantonal des Beaux Arts de Lausanne in 2001. She was a Leverhulme Special Research Fellow at Duncan of Jordanstone College of Art in Dundee from 1998–2001.

The Sabin Brothers, Edinburgh, 1998, is one of a series of photographs collectively titled *Young Musicians*. The images feature children in the act of playing a musical instrument. McMurdo has, however, digitally manipu-lated the images to erase the instrument from the scene, leaving only the pensive child, caught transfixed by something now unknowable to us.

Her recent works *Boy with Bubble* and *Lifestyle Affects Appearance, Bio-Medical Galleries*, 2000, were made at the Science Museum, London and capture children enthralled by the displays. The boy in question appears utterly captivated by the object of his contem-plation and his at-oneness with the object is heightened by the way in which the image tends to suggest that he is in fact located inside rather than outside the bubble – an object for scrutiny himself. Like McMurdo's previous work with children, these images suggest notions of the development of the ego, the awareness of self and the creation of a psychic world. They tend to highlight the emergence of a barrier between the inner and outer self. **KB**

'Even when the secret of Photoshop and digital media is revealed to us, the technical feats do not suffice to explain away the uncanniness of McMurdo's pictures.' Gilda Williams

REFERENCE

Wendy McMurdo, Centre for Photo-graphy, University of Salamanca (2nd edition), 2001

Boy with Bubble, The Science Museum 2000
c-type print · courtesy the artist and Andrew Mummery Gallery, London

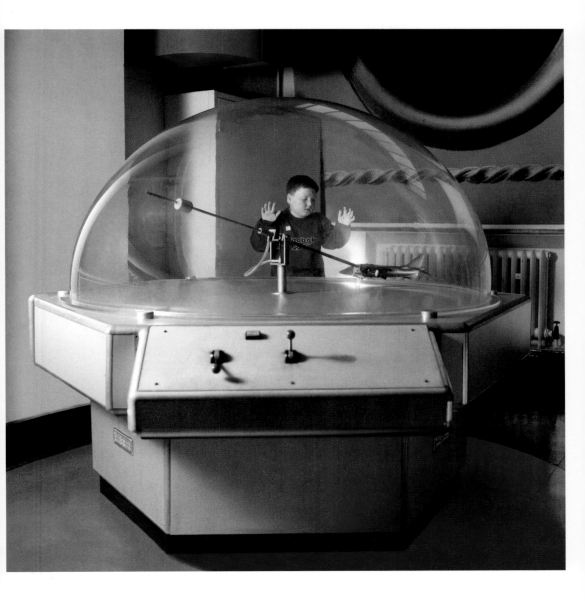

Janice **McNab**

Born in Aberfeldy in 1964, Janice McNab studied at Edinburgh School of Art and on the MA course at Glasgow School of Art where she completed her studies in 1997. In 1998 McNab had a solo exhibition at the Collective Gallery, Edinburgh. She has completed a number of studio residencies including the Glasgow City of Culture residency in Vienna in 1990, the Wurlitzer Foundation's studio residency in New Mexico in 1998 and the Scottish Arts Council studio residency in Amsterdam in 2000. 2001 sees a solo exhibition at Tramway, Glasgow. She lives and works in Edinburgh.

Recent paintings by Janice McNab have portrayed individuals whose sensitivity to everyday chemicals leaves them at the margins of society. These individuals' health has been permanently damaged as a result of accidental overexposure to chemicals such as organophosphates that are used industrially in agriculture, and domestically for pest control or in timber treatments. McNab's paintings are often produced from flash-lit photographs that illuminate her subjects in a harsh, bright light against the domestic confines that they are often unable to leave.

Jean made micro-chips for 24 years, 2000, and *Anne*, 2001, are paintings that portray women who worked at The National Semiconductor factory in Greenock making electronic components. Such work involves the daily use of dangerous chemicals such as sulphuric, hydrofluoric and chromic acid. It has been claimed that environmental conditions within the factory have caused long term health problems for former employees including reproductive problems and cancers. RT

REFERENCE

Janice McNab, The Collective Gallery, Edinburgh, 1999

Jean made microchips for 24 years 2000
oil on board · courtesy the artist and doggerfisher, Edinburgh

Alan **Michael**

Born in Glasgow in 1967, Alan Michael studied Painting at Duncan of Jordanstone College of Art and Design in Dundee and on the MA course at Glasgow School of Art, which he completed in 1998. In 1999 he exhibited, together with Alex Frost, at the Collective Gallery, Edinburgh. He is a former member of the committee at Transmission Gallery and has exhibited in group exhibitions at the CCA and Tramway, Glasgow, The Showroom, London, and at the Three Month Gallery, Liverpool. In 1999 he completed a residency at Asterides-Systeme Friche, Marseilles. He lives and works in Glasgow.

Alan Michael's paintings and drawings are comprised of collages of obscure reference points intended to create new, fictional understandings of our cultural history.

Misty in Roots, 2001, is a proposal for a magazine cover. The work takes its name from the legendary British dub band of the 1980's. Household pot plants frame a series of references: the American all-girl folk band, The Roches, Demetrio Tsafendas (who in 1996 assassinated Henrik Verwoed, the architect of South African apartheid), the Japanese author Yukio Mishima and Gunter Sachs (the photographer, astrologist and former husband of Brigitte Bardot).

Community Cinema, 2000, is adapted from a poster advertising a public art project by Rirkrit Tiravanija, *Community Cinema for a quiet intersection (against Oldenburg)*, held in Glasgow in 1999. Tiravanija's work involved street screenings of the audience's favourite films: *The Jungle Book*, *Casablanca*, *It's a Wonderful Life* and *A Bug's Life*. Michael appropriated text advertising the screening and populated the remaining space with a series of sprawling nudes copied from paintings by the contemporary American Realist painter Philip Pearlstein.

Sticky Fingers, 1997, is a drawing of the Rolling Stones album cover as it was released in 1971 in Spain then under Fascist control. The famous 'zipper' design by Andy Warhol, used for the cover in the rest of the world, was deemed unsuitable by General Franco's administration and replaced with the image of a human hand emerging from a tin of treacle. **RT**

Misty in Roots 2001
acrylic and pencil on paper · courtesy the artist

Misty in Roots in Summer

Demetrio Tsafendas' Story

Yukio MiShima in The Sea of Peaür

BLSS MESS

Andrew **Miller**

Born in Dartington, Devon in 1969, Andrew Miller studied Photography at Glasgow School of Art where he later completed an MA in 1993. In 1994, he was selected for *New Art in Scotland* at the CCA, Glasgow and Aberdeen Art Gallery and *New Contemporaries*. In 1997–98 he worked with artist Richard Wright and architects RMJM on the redevelopment of the Tron Theatre, Glasgow. He had a solo show at the Percy Miller Gallery, London in 2000.

The relationship between people, objects and places, specifically how context leads to an understanding of function, has been central to Miller's work with photography, sculpture and drawings. His interest in architecture and design has led him to work on several 'cross-over' projects, such as the design of a table for the 'Please Touch' furniture collection commissioned during Glasgow's Year of Architecture and Design in 1999.

Miller's *Nonagon* and *Passing Time* are distinct but related works, which together prompt a consideration of the correlation between plan and volume, between two and three dimensions. *Passing Time* is a seating structure, comprised of nine separable 'units', each of which is mobile and capable of containing other objects or materials. The configuration of the units is open – they can either be grouped together as an enclosure, for use by a self-defined group, or scattered separately, their connection and association between their users left implicit. Miller's photographic diptych, *Terry and June* also affords us two distinct readings of the same person with the same object: only the positioning differs from one to the other. These works encourage us to consider how we interpret the function of an object and how our responses and value judgements are coloured by that interpretation. KB

Passing Time (foreground) and **Nonogon** 1996
wall painting; veneered MDF, basketball · courtesy the artist

Victoria **Morton**

Born in Glasgow in 1971, Victoria Morton studied Painting at Glasgow School of Art and subsequently on the MA course, which she completed in 1995. She was selected for *New Art in Scotland* at the CCA, Glasgow in 1994, and Aberdeen Art Gallery in 1995, and was included in *Loaded: A Contemporary View of British Painting* at the Ikon Gallery, Birmingham in 1996. Morton had a solo exhibition at Transmission Gallery, Glasgow in 1996, the Changing Room, Stirling in 1999 and Sadie Coles HQ, London in 2001. As well as exhibiting her own work, she makes collaborative work as a member of *Elizabeth Go* with Hayley Tompkins, Sue Tompkins, Sarah Tripp and Cathy Wilkes and is a member of the band 'Suckle'. Between 1996 and 2001 she was a lecturer at Duncan of Jordanstone College of Art & Design in Dundee. She lives and works in Glasgow.

Although she has produced works in other media, Victoria Morton's practice is primarily that of painting. Her sometimes fresh, sometimes laboured works seem to hover between abstraction and representation, often containing just sufficient visual information to call to mind remembered images. Highly atmospheric, Morton's works develop through a process of working that is more interested in how the final piece might feel than simply how it will look. She brings together colours, forms, textures and lines suggested to her by a broad range of sources, from fashion and design to high art. The resultant works, with intriguing, evocative titles give only scant clues as to their possible origin, often based around the human figure.

Morton's works tend to be built up in layers and sections, creating a sense of space in the finished painting. Early works often used a variety of means of applying the paint, from spraying to the use of hard objects. Most recent works such as *Plus and Minus* and *Painting for Mary* have developed from her earlier organic forms to show more geometric patterns and forms, while continuing to express an interest in the associative power of colour. **KB**

REFERENCE
DECAPODA, Changing Room, Stirling, 1999

Painting for Mary 2000
oil on canvas · courtesy the artist, The Modern Institute and Sadie Coles HQ, London

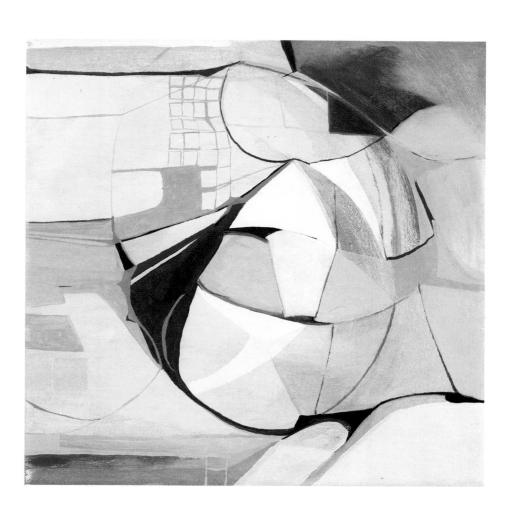

Toby **Paterson**

Born in Glasgow in 1974, Toby Paterson studied painting at Glasgow School of Art graduating in 1995. Between 1996 and 1998 he was a member of the committee at Transmission Gallery, Glasgow. His first solo exhibition was in 1999 at The Modern Institute, Glasgow. In 2001 he participated in several group exhibitions including *Circles #4* at ZKM, Karlsruhe, and *Beyond* at Dundee Contemporary Arts. Paterson recently completed a major public sculpture commission in Royston, Glasgow, for The Centre. He lives and works in Glasgow.

Toby Paterson is best known for his paintings of architectural features. Paterson's paintings often depict concrete buildings not as a critique of the Modern movement but painted with an affection and enthusiasm for the urban landscape in which he lives. Paterson's understanding of such structures is heightened by his interest in skateboarding. Paterson sees cities and buildings as a series of micro-spaces to navigate – a series of surfaces to isolate and present in his paintings. Art galleries are not simply places in which to place his work but provide a location in which he makes work directly onto the walls; to draw and paint his repertoire of diving boards, military defences, pavilions, ramps, shelters, showrooms and staircases.

Recent works have been inspired by the works of the architect (and painter) Le Corbusier and the painter (and architect) Victor Pasmore. *Science and Art*, 2001, is Paterson's impression of an unrealised plan of Pasmore's, from 1955, for a museum of art and science in Chicago dedicated to the physicist Enrico Fermi. **RT**

'Toby Paterson paints in light. The feeling of his compositions is that of a shutter releasing on a perfect sunny day. The image is centred, focussed: the background falls away. This is what he will make memorable: idealised depictions of Modernist architecture, precisely rendered.'
Sarah Lowndes in 'Toby Paterson', *Static Utopia*

REFERENCE

Toby Paterson, The Modern Institute, Glasgow, 2001

Science and Art 2001
acrylic on perspex · courtesy the artist and The Modern Institute

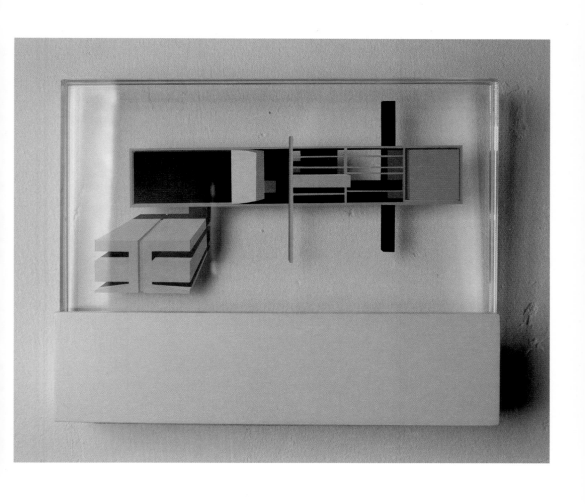

Mary **Redmond**

Born in Glasgow in 1972, Mary Redmond studied in the Environmental Art Department at Glasgow School of Art and subsequently on the MA course, completing her studies in 1998. She has participated in several group exhibitions in Scotland and abroad including *Girls' High* at the Old Fruitmarket, Glasgow, 1996, and *Red Marauder*, Tramway, Glasgow, 2000. She had her first solo exhibition at The Modern Institute, Glasgow in 1999. 2002 sees the completion of a major public artwork commissioned by the Centre, Glasgow, for Scotland's first National Park, Loch Lomond and the Trossachs.

In much the same way as a painter might combine colour, texture and line, Mary Redmond brings together found objects and materials in a way that emphasises their aesthetic qualities. Her works assume an intriguing quality, hovering between the strange and the familiar. They pull together divergent substances, from industrial materials such as metal fencing or plastic piping, to delicate, brightly coloured fabrics.

Works such as *Shufflebagger*, 2000, demonstrate an eye for both colour and composition. Its basis of a discarded plastic seat, of the type found in many public buildings, reduces something normally experienced as mundane and functional to colour and form, a support to which other materials are added. Her essentially abstract works tend to share an ability to evoke the human body, by means of the regular incorporation of objects that are suggestive of its form, such as furniture and clothing. KB

Shufflebagger 2000
polypropeleyne, plywood, acrylic paint, tape, cord and steel bracket ·
courtesy the artist and The Modern Institute

Carol **Rhodes**

Born in Edinburgh in 1959, Rhodes studied painting at Glasgow School of Art graduating in 1982. She had her first major solo exhibition at Tramway, Glasgow following a residency there in 2000. Rhodes is a former member of the committee at Transmission Gallery and she has exhibited in many group exhibitions in Britain including *New Art in Scotland*, at the CCA, Glasgow in 1994 and Aberdeen Art Gallery in 1995. In 1999 she was shortlisted for the prestigious Jerwood Painting Prize and in 2000 she participated in the *British Art Show 5*. She lives and works in Glasgow and teaches at Glasgow School of Art.

Carol Rhodes creates small, intimate paintings of fictional landscapes. The spaces are always slightly familiar and yet are derived from images and her recollection of different places that she reconfigures. The landscapes appear desolate and yet always depict places that have been dramatically shaped by people.

Carpark, Canal, 1995, and *Service Station*, 1998, depict roadside environments that have been presented by Rhodes with an exacting economy of oil paint applied, almost like a thin veneer, onto board.

More recent works, such as *Runway*, 2001, portray landscape from an elevation that we can only experience from the air. The locations Rhodes pictures are heavily marked by the elements and by man-made earthmoving equipment. These environments appear to be insignificant locations and yet they retain a calm beauty we normally associate with abstract painting. **RT**

'As the eye recedes from the land all parts of what is viewed are perfected. Rugged outcrops into the sea are smoothed away into the generalised sweep of the shore. Roads lose all but their grandest curves and hills make a gentle round protrusion in the smooth surface of the world. The earth's variegated cover simplifies into broad areas of one subtly modelled hue and the sky's activity into a single tone.'
Jane Lee in *Carol Rhodes*

REFERENCE

Carol Rhodes, Tramway, 2000

Runway 2001
oil on board · courtesy the artist and Andrew Mummery Gallery, London

Craig **Richardson**

Born in Glasgow in 1966, Richardson studied in the Environmental Art Department at Glasgow School of Art, where he was also one of the first students on the MA course, from 1988–1990. He was a committee member at Transmission Gallery in 1991. Richardson participated in several important exhibitions in the early 1990s, including *Self-Conscious State* at the Third Eye Centre, Glasgow in 1990, *Windfall*, Glasgow in 1991, *Guilt by Association* at the Irish Museum of Modern Art in 1992, *Institute of Cultural Anxiety* at the ICA, London and *Riviera* at the Oriel Mostyn Gallery, Llandudno in 1994. Chisenhale Gallery, London presented an exhibition by Richardson and Christine Borland in 1993. His work has subsequently been included in a number of group exhibitions in Europe, including *Circles #4* at ZKM, Karlsruhe in 2001. He has lived in London since 1993 and now teaches Fine Art at Oxford Brookes University.

REFERENCE

Christine Borland and Craig Richardson, Chisenhale Gallery, 1993

Richardson's work explores the languages of control and instruction, both visual and verbal. His work with signs, symbols and text references a broad range of mechanisms for information and warning. In text works such as *The Unfolding*, 1993, he exploits both a specific use of colour, in this instance the application of black text to a vibrant yellow wall to call to mind danger signs, and the associations of language, in a series of phrases which seem contradictory. Combinations such as 'Beneficial Massacre' and 'Pleasant Extinction' imply the now familiar though uncomfortable use of such euphemisms as 'ethnic cleansing' and 'friendly fire'.

In tandem with his work with text and symbols, Richardson has realised a series of object-based pieces, which in common with his other work convey a characteristic sense of unease. One of a series of what Richardson himself has referred to as 'delinquent weapons' *I have made a mistake and now I must fix it*, 1994, presents us with what at first appears to be a collection of found objects, arms and instruments of torture. On closer inspection, however, the objects reveal a home-made quality. They have clearly been fashioned from materials familiar from other usage, some of which we may recognise. The objects, presented in a museum-like neutral style, have clearly come about through a purposeful transformation of an innocuous, often domestic material, into something much more sinister. These objects are rich with a sense of violence conceived and an intent to control, illustrative of Richardson' interest in the enforcement of what is allowed and what is not. **KB**

I have made a mistake and now I must fix it 1994
wood, metal, paint · courtesy the artist

Julie **Roberts**

Born in Fflint, Wales in 1963, Julie Roberts studied in Wrexham School of Art, St Martin's School of Art, London and subsequently undertook the MA at Glasgow School of Art from 1988–90. Roberts participated in the exhibition *Windfall* in 1991. Her first solo exhibitions were at the CCA, Glasgow and the James Hockey Gallery, Farnham in 1992. Since then her work has been included in numerous exhibitions internationally, including the 1995 Venice Biennale. She is currently based in New York. Her most recent work was exhibited at the Pier Art Centre, Orkney in summer 2001.

Julie Roberts works with images of places and objects that are loaded with meaning, rich in significance. Using a process first developed with her early 1990s paintings of medical instruments and apparatus, Roberts undertakes extensive research and enquiry prior to commencing a painting. The starting point for her work is often the museum, historical collections and artefacts, where meaning has accrued to objects through time and changes in technology, beliefs and attitudes. The objects on which her focus comes to rest are, however, presented to us entirely abstracted from their context, floating in the centre of a field of solid colour.

The resultant works, devoid of any direct representation of the human body, tend to emphasise its manipulation, and seem to suggest more malicious than benevolent intent. They each assert a concern for the points of connection between the individual and the institution, for the ways in which the latter deals with the former. Roberts' paintings, such as *Restraining Coat II (female)* combine a sense of museum-like objectivity and gravitas with a chilling awareness of the uses and implications of the depicted object. Removed from a connection with the human form for which it is intended, the object itself becomes a sinister symbol of control. As with so many of Roberts' works, the stark, isolated object evokes the full extent of its social and cultural significance, beyond the purely medical. **KB**

REFERENCES

Julie Roberts, Glasgow Print Studio, 1996

Julie Roberts, Third Eye Centre, Glasgow, 1992

Restraining Coat II (female) 1995
oil and acrylic on canvas · courtesy the artist and Aberdeen Art Gallery

David **Shrigley**

Born in Macclesfield in 1968, Shrigley studied in the Environmental Art Department at Glasgow School of Art graduating in 1991. He had his first solo exhibition at Transmission Gallery, Glasgow in 1995. He has exhibited in many group exhibitions in Britain and abroad including *New Art in Scotland*, at the CCA, Glasgow in 1994, and Aberdeen Art Gallery in 1995 and *Open Country* in Lausanne in 2001. In 1994 Shrigley founded Armpit Press. He has published fourteen collections of his drawings and in 1999 contributed a weekly drawing to the Independent on Sunday. In 2001 Shrigley participated in the *British Art Show 5*, and was shortlisted for the inaugural Beck's Futures Prize. 2001 sees a major retrospective exhibition of his work at Bard College, New York. He lives and works in Glasgow.

David Shrigley's absurd photographs, drawings, paintings and sculpture operate in a long tradition of comic and art illustration offering a different perspective on the human condition. Shrigley's works, however funny are often underlined by a bleak perspective on life.

Imagine the Green is Red, 1997, was first made for the Tate Gallery in Liverpool as one of a number of commissions made whilst the gallery was being redeveloped, presented as part of an insert in Tate Magazine. Like many of Shrigley's works it is made in Kelvingrove Park in Glasgow, close to where the artist lived and is one of a number of works that offers an alternative view of civic space. Whilst the notion of transforming this green expanse into one that is red is comic, another work, *Red Kermit*, made the following year is more sinister. The photograph presents a child's toy abandoned next to some water. The presenter of the Muppet Show, fabricated from red rather than green felt, is transformed into a demonic character. **RT**

REFERENCES

Grip, Pocketbooks, Edinburgh, 2000

Why we got the sack from the Museum, Redstone Press, London, 1998

Blank Page and Other pages, The Modern Institute, Glasgow, 1998

Err, Bookworks, London, 1996

Imagine the Green is Red 1997
photograph · courtesy the artist and Stephen Friedman

Ross **Sinclair**

Born in Glasgow in 1966, Sinclair studied in the Environmental Art Department at Glasgow School of Art, where he subsequently completed the MFA course in 1992. He had his first solo exhibition, *Fanclub*, at Stills Gallery, Edinburgh in 1992 and was subsequently awarded the Scottish Arts Council residency in Amsterdam in 1994. Sinclair has exhibited internationally with solo exhibitions *Real Life Rocky Mountain* at the CCA, Glasgow in 1996 and *A Dream of the Hamnavoe Free State* at the Pier Arts Centre, Stromness in 1998. A further solo exhibition, *Journey to the End of the World*, took place at the Fruitmarket Gallery, Edinburgh in 1999, and in 2000, at Aspex Gallery, Portsmouth. In 1997 he participated in *Glasgow*, Kunsthalle Bern, in 1998, *Nettverk Glasgow*, Museum for Samtidskunst in Oslo and in 2001, *Circles 4#* at ZKM, Karlsruhe. In 1998 he was awarded the Paul Hamlyn Foundation award to Artists. His most recent solo exhibition, *Fortress Real Life (Peckham)*, took place at the South London Gallery in 2001. He lives and works in Glasgow and teaches part-time at Glasgow School of Art.

REFERENCES

Real Life and How to Live It, Fruitmarket Gallery, Edinburgh, 2000

Real Life, Centre for Contemporary Arts, Glasgow, 1996

Using the mass-produced forms of ephemeral promotional items such as posters and badges, Ross Sinclair's works of the early 1990s were characterised by an opposition between individual identity and corporate, global homogenisation. In a poster work in Glasgow in 1990, for example, Sinclair paired the City's title as 'Capital of Culture' with the inverse 'Culture of Capital'.

Sinclair's work has often demonstrated his interest in public performance, in the presentation of an (his) individual character in the public realm. Several works have involved Sinclair's actual presence, his direct engagement with the audience. In 1994 he had the words 'Real Life' tattooed in black across his shoulders, a phrase which has become a constant theme in many of his works. With all the visual qualities and associative powers of a strong brand identity, it recurs throughout works in video, installation and photography. Asking us what constitutes the real in a society where so much is rendered inauthentic, Sinclair continues to explore the political and the personal ramifications of the culture in which we are involved.

His *Portable Studio Real Life*, 1995, is one of a number of works based on an ad hoc stage crowded with the effects of a performance – posters, t-shirts, beer bottles, music equipment. It combines an express commitment to individual achievement and aspiration – referenced, as so often in Sinclair's work, by pop music - with an awareness of the certainty of failure. His trademark, often humorous hand-painted t-shirts bear, among others things, song titles, snappy soundbites and smart slogans, such as 'EMPTV'. KB

Portable Studio Real Life 1995
painted t-shirts, DVD and monitor · courtesy the artist

IN THE MEANTIME BEFORE
FAILURE STUDIO REAL LIFE
AT ALPENMILCHZENTRALE
UBER ALLES
FUT UREISM
LEAVE IT TO BEAVER
PASSIVE SCHOOL OF CULTURAL INERTIA
CENTER FOR CONTEMPORARY ANGST
TV
FUCK ALL Y'ALL
DEAD AIR
JESUS IS A WOMAN TOO
GALLERY OF MODERN MYOPIA
STUSSY
STAR SPANGLD BANNE
WAR IS OVER IF
REAL LIFE

Smith/Stewart

Born in Manchester in 1968, Stephanie Smith studied at The Slade School of Fine Art, London and the Rijksakademie van Beeldende Kunsten, Amsterdam. Eddie Stewart was born in Belfast in 1961 and studied at Glasgow School of Art and the Rijksakademie van Beeldende Kunsten, Amsterdam. Both artists completed their studies in 1993 and participated separately in *New Art in Scotland*, CCA, Glasgow in 1994, and Aberdeen Art Gallery in 1995. Smith/Stewart have been working collaboratively since 1993. They have exhibited extensively in Britain and abroad. Their first major joint exhibition was at Tramway in 1995. Smith/Stewart have participated in a number of important group exhibitions involving artists from Scotland including, *Glasgow* Kunsthalle Bern, in 1997 and *Open Country*, in Lausanne. In 1999 they had a solo exhibition at the Kunstmuseum Luzern and, in 2000, Portikus, Frankfurt. Smith and Stewart live and work in Glasgow.

Smith and Stewart's video installation work is characterised by shared interests in identity, language and the body. Accordingly the mouth is a recurring motif. In *Sustain*, a video installation from 1995, Smith is recorded, repeatedly biting Stewart, covering his torso with red marks. Whilst in *Part*, 1998, a monitor displays the results of a camera repeatedly entering a mouth. The person tries to speak but the camera prevents them.

Dual from 1997 sees a continuation of the artists' preoccupation with language and the body. A monitor displays the artists' attempts to write with both hands simultaneously, together. Smith, who is left-handed, and Stewart, who is right-handed, each force the other's non-writing hand to inscribe their name. In this way each artist forces the other to produce a signature. The work poses questions about how identities are established for us rather than us establishing them for ourselves. RT

REFERENCES

Sustain, The Showroom, London, 1996

Smith/ Stewart, The Fruitmarket Gallery, Edinburgh 1998

Smith/ Stewart, Videoarbeiten, Kunstmuseum Luzern and Portikus, Frankfurt 1999

Dual 1997
DVD on monitor, table · courtesy the artists

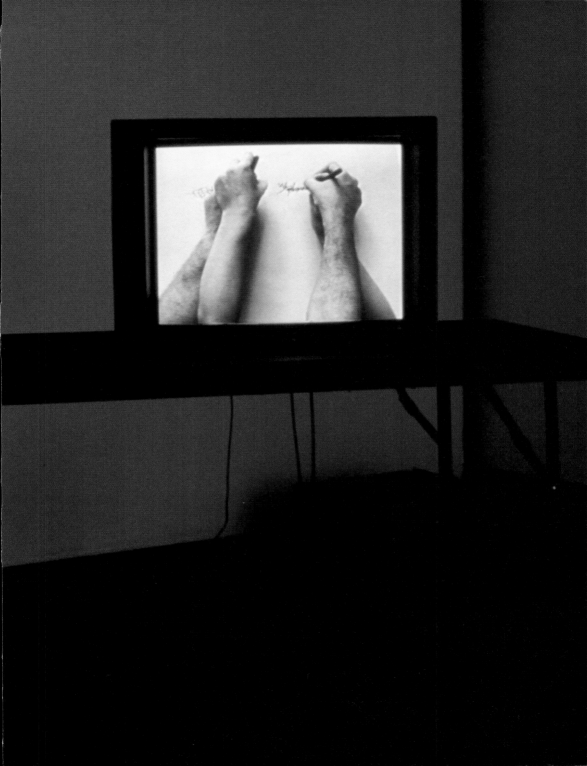

Bryndis **Snæbjörnsdóttir**

Born in Reykjavik, Bryndis Snæbjörnsdóttir studied first at the University of Iceland before studying in the Environmental Art Department and on the MA course at Glasgow School of Art where she completed her studies in 1994. Her first solo exhibition was at Gallery One in Reykjavik in 1993. She has subsequently had solo exhibitions with the Henry Moore Institute (as part of its external programme 'Here and Now') in 1998 and at Portfolio Gallery, Edinburgh in 1999. In 1999 she co-organised *If I Ruled the World …* at The Living Art Museum, Reykjavik, and at the CCA, Glasgow in 2000. Between 1998 and 2001 she taught at Glasgow School of Art and in 2001 began a residency at Qaqortoq, Greenland.

In her photography, sound installations and object making Bryndis Snæbjörnsdóttir is concerned with ambiguity and apparent contradiction. She is best known for her photographic series *Building a Balcony*, 1999. The work documented a hazardous journey made by Snæbjörnsdóttir and her partner across an uninhabited, desolate island situated in the North West of Iceland. Large black and white landscape photographs of the romantic terrain are juxtaposed with smaller, colour images of herself, her, partner, their activity and evidence of other animal occupation within the bleak landscape. The different images appear to undermine each other. Describing another, sound and photographic work, *Model for a parapet*, 1998, resulting from a walk in Scotland, Snæbjörnsdóttir wrote 'I am fascinated by the capacity of the photograph to capture the "real" and consciously "freeze" the moment. It opens up a dialogue between the moments before and after the image was "removed". The ambiguity of the "before" and "after" is the key to the viewer's own access to the work … I am interested in extending the moment beyond any sense of seizure. This generosity and expandability of the photographic medium echoes the process and the linearity that is the walk itself.'

but not waiting … and an untitled sculptural work, both from 1995, offer different representations of presence and absence. From one aspect these works appear as positive plaster casts of an upturned jug on a tray, from another as negative casts. They appear simultaneously as both full and as empty vessels. RT

Untitled 1995
plaster · courtesy the artist and Aberdeen Art Gallery

Simon **Starling**

Born in Epsom in 1967, Starling studied at Nottingham Polytechnic and on Glasgow School of Art's MA course which he completed in 1992. Whilst a committee member of Transmission Gallery, Glasgow, he had his first solo exhibition at London's Showroom Gallery in 1995. He has subsequently had several solo shows in major public galleries including, in 2001, the Secession, Vienna and Camden Arts Centre, London and in 1998, The Moderna Museet, Stockholm. Starling has also participated in a number of significant group exhibitions including the *British Art Show 5* and *Manifesta 3*, Ljubliana, both 2000. In 1999 Simon Starling was awarded the Blinky Palermo Prize, The Henry Moore Sculpture Fellowship at Duncan of Jordanstone College of Art, Dundee and the Paul Hamlyn Foundation award to Artists. Starling lives and works in Glasgow.

REFERENCES

Simon Starling, Camden Arts Centre, London/ John Hansard Gallery, Southampton, 2001

Simon Starling, Moderna Museet, Stockholm, 1999

Simon Starling, Galerie Für Zeitgenossiche Kunst, Liepzig 1999

Simon Starling explores the ways in which objects become identifiable and are subsequently classified or validated. His projects have often tracked the process of transformation from one object or substance to another, for example constructing a small boat from the wood of a disused museum vitrine or casting replica beer cans from the metal of a chair. Starling compares his position to that of the nineteenth century amateur scientist or inventor as he reintroduces craft and amateur enthusiasms to contemporary manufacturing or classification.

Rescued Rhododendrons, 2000, charts Starling's expedition to return a number plants introduced to Scotland in the eighteenth century to the place where they were first introduced to Europe. Rhododendrons were first planted in Scotland by landowners as decorative plants, they hybridised and flourished and are now being removed from managed estates as they are not 'indigenous.' Starling resolved to transport some specimens from Elrick Hill, outside Aberdeen, to Parque Los Alcornocales, in the south of Spain, from where they were first introduced into widespread cultivation in Europe in 1763 by the Swedish botanist Claes Alstroemer. Starling's two screen projected video, documenting the transit of plant specimens is played both forward and in reverse, positive and negative, compressing several hundred years of botanical experiments into a few minutes of footage. *Rescued Rhododendrons* follows Starling's first film work *Short Story, Brief History*, 1999, commissioned for the opening of Dundee Contemporary Arts. RT

Rescued Rhododendrons 2000
DVD projections · courtesy the artist and The Modern Institute

Joanne **Tatham** and Tom **O'Sullivan**

Born in West Yorkshire in 1971, Joanne Tatham studied at Duncan of Jordanstone College of Art and Design and on the MA course at Glasgow School of Art graduating in 1995. Tom O'Sullivan was born in Norwich in 1967 and studied at Leeds University and on the MA course at Glasgow School of Art graduating in 1994. Tatham and O'Sullivan have been working collaboratively in Glasgow since 1995. Their first joint exhibition was at the Three Month Gallery, Liverpool in 1997 and they have exhibited extensively across Britain. In 2001 they exhibited in the Berlin Biennale and have a solo exhibition at Tramway in Glasgow. They live and work in Glasgow.

Joanne Tatham and Tom O'Sullivan's work is made in the tradition of conceptual art in that it concerns itself with questioning the parameters of what can be considered to be 'art'.

Whilst conceptual art is usually associated with the de-materialisation of the art-object, installations by Tatham and O'Sullivan such as *Resurrection with three forms*, 1998, utilise amateur craft skills to create objects that are very physical and force the viewer to engage with them. Their works quote pre-existing languages, not just from art history, but from popular music and archetypal design as they idealistically attempt to communicate very directly with a broad audience.

Art for People, a poster designed by Tom O'Sullivan in 1996 for Transmission Gallery and the show which it advertised, was made at a particular moment in Glasgow when contemporary practice within the city was seen to be shunned by officialdom. A collection established by the then Director of Glasgow Museums (as the Glasgow Museum of Modern Art) failed to represent internationally recognised contemporary practice within Scotland. *Art for People* was the first of a now annual 'members show' held at the artists-run gallery where the large membership are invited to exhibit work without curatorial selection. **RT**

REFERENCE

The Glamour, Joanne Tatham and Tom O'Sullivan with Will Bradley, Transmission Gallery, 2001

Resurrection with three forms (detail) 1998
tie-dyed banner, ceramic objects, black plinths · courtesy the artist and The Modern Institute

James **Thornhill**

Born in Hampshire, 1967, James Thornhill studied at Bournemouth and Poole College of Art and Design and the Frei Universität für Bildende Kunst, Hamburg before studying at Glasgow School of Art where he completed the MA course in 2001. In 1994 and 1995 he participated in *New Art in Scotland*, CCA, Glasgow, and Aberdeen Art Gallery. In 1995 Thornhill organised a number of group shows in a semi-derelict Glasgow tenement and subsequently organised a large group show, *Notell Hotel*, in a hotel room (together with Graham Fagen and Hilary Stirling). In 1999 he presented a series of solo exhibitions at his flat in Dennistoun, Glasgow as Ready Steady Made. In 2001 he completes a residency at the Ecole Regionale des Beaux Arts de Nantes. Since 2000 Thornhill has also worked collaboratively with Michelle Naismith as 'a Love Laboratory'. He lives and works in Glasgow.

James Thornhill's sculpture and video works revisit the recent past. They have a melancholic feel and attempt to articulate a sense of anger, boredom and loss. Thornhill uses 'found' objects that he transforms and yet allows to hold a ghostly presence of their previous use.

LETTER-TWOCKER (seven sites: 5 consonants / 2 vowels), 1999, is one of a series of works that comprise three dimensional texts, constructed from plastic, metal, wood and neon shop signage. The work reads 'Liberty' reflecting the fact that Thornhill has taken the letters from another source in order to reinvent them. The 'TWOCKER' from the title refers to the police terminology for theft (ie. 'taken without consent'). Other works made in this way read 'saturn', '(un)bounded' and 'wasteland'.

Counter – Word, 2000, is similarly composed from existing signage. Thornhill found the outdated 'Mecca' sign in a derelict bingo hall in Glasgow's east end. The writing is reversed, inverting the sign's purpose. **RT**

LETTER-TWOCKER (Seven sites:
5 consonants / 2 vowels) 1999
found signage · courtesy the artist

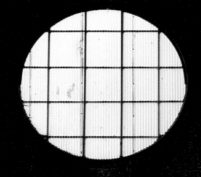

Graeme **Todd**

Born in Glasgow in 1962, Graeme Todd studied Painting at Duncan of Jordanstone College of Art and Design in Dundee graduating in 1985. In 1990 he participated in *Scatter; New Scottish Art* at the Third Eye Centre, Glasgow. He had his first solo exhibition at the Seagate Gallery, Dundee, in 1989. In 2000, following an IAAB residency in Basel, he had a solo show at the Fruitmarket Gallery, Edinburgh and Leeds Metropolitan University Gallery. He has exhibited extensively in Britain and abroad. He lives and works in Edinburgh and teaches at Edinburgh College of Art.

Graeme Todd's paintings appear to draw from a wide variety of sources. His loose compositions of lines, dots and splashes sealed by a warm, transparent lacquer veneer could appear to be informed by astronomical diagrams, fifteenth century Japanese ink drawings and by nineteenth century Romantic paintings of the sublime.

In paintings such as *Lovecraft*, amidst layers of painted marks, applied in oil, acrylic ink, and pastel, details of clouds and foliage are clearly visible. In Todd's paintings accumulated marks and traditions merge under transparent varnish surfaces to form condensed histories of landscape depiction. **RT**

REFERENCE

Mount Hiddenabyss, Graeme Todd, Fruitmarket Gallery, Edinburgh, 2000

Lovecraft 1997
oil, acrylic ink, pastel and lacquer on board · courtesy the artist and the Scottish National Gallery of Modern Art

Hayley **Tompkins**

Born in Leighton Buzzard in 1971, Hayley Tompkins studied painting and on the MA course at Glasgow School of Art where she completed her studies in 1998. In 1999 she exhibited, together with Sue Tompkins, at Transmission Gallery. In 2000, she had a solo exhibition at The Modern Institute, Glasgow. She has exhibited extensively in Scotland, and abroad. Since 1997 she has made collaborative work together with Victoria Morton, Sue Tompkins and Sarah Tripp as Elizabeth Go. She lives and works in Glasgow.

Hayley Tompkins creates works on paper that she sees as being half-way between painting and drawing. Executed quickly and as components of large series, recent works consist of a mixture of intuitive abstract mark making and recognisable forms, texts and dates. The paintings are intended to convey an attitude or a particular state of mind.

Beautiful Boy, 1995, consists of six meticulously produced figurative paintings first exhibited in 'The Persistence of Painting' at the CCA, Glasgow in the same year. The details identified and reproduced as paintings by Tompkins were taken from magazines. More recent, often untitled, works on paper are produced with lighter washes of watercolour in order to retain a greater impression of spontaneity and experiment. Specific references are contained within these works but are left unacknowledged to allow the viewer to create their own relationship with the painted surface. **RT**

Work from **Parade** 2001
watercolour on paper · courtesy the artist and The Modern Institute

Donald **Urquhart**

Born in Bankfoot, Perthshire in 1959, Donald Urquhart studied at Edinburgh College of Art. His solo project *Grey Weighted Notes* was presented in An Lanntair, Stornoway, Talbot Rice Gallery, Edinburgh and Aberdeen Art Gallery in 1997–8. He was artist in residence at Grizedale Forest in 1998 and in 1999 he undertook a residency at the Irish Musuem of Modern Art in Dublin. Much of the work that resulted from the residency became the exhibition *Fields* shown in St Andrews, Kilkenny, Derry and Stavanger in 2001. After several years in Glasgow, Urquhart now lives in Edinburgh.

Our relationship to landscape has been a constant fascination for Donald Urquhart, both in terms of a direct response to the natural environment, but also and increasingly through the eyes of the past.

Dark Idyll I and *II*, 1997, share with much of Urquhart's other work the use of imagery of the natural environment gleaned from existent material. His interest in how we perceive our environs has led him to look at earlier depictions of the landscape, in this case the point of origin is a series of nineteenth century engravings of wooded landscape, a typically idyllic vision. His recent paintings have repeatedly taken the form of multi-panel pieces, often diptychs, emphasising the depicted material as fragmentary and partial. **KB**

'Over centuries the art of depicting landscape has accrued so many layers of myth, significance and memory that the challenge today is to find a means to make any representation of landscape relevant again. Confronting this issue in his paintings, Urquhart states that they can be seen as rational elements against the mythology of the wilderness.'
Francis McKee in *A Day Like Any Other*
Solvberget, Stavanger Kulturhus, 2000

REFERENCE

Donald Urquhart: Fields, Butler Gallery, Kilkenny, 2001

Interrupted Landscape 1 1999
oil on canvas · courtesy the artist

Clara **Ursitti**

Born in Toronto, 1968, Clara Ursitti studied at York University, Toronto and on the MA course at Glasgow School of Art which she completed in 1995. She participated in *New Art in Scotland*, CCA, Glasgow, in 1994 and Aberdeen Art Gallery in 1995. Her first solo exhibitions were in 1997 at the Collective Gallery, Edinburgh and Transmission Gallery, Glasgow. She has exhibited extensively in Britain and internationally. In 1998 she completed an artist's residency at Tower Studio, Melbourne University. She lives and works in Glasgow.

In 1993 Clara Ursitti began working with the biochemist George Dodd to re-create her own body scent. The resulting work was exhibited at the CCA in Glasgow. Following this investigation Ursitti established an international dating agency, 'Pheromone Link', based upon scent rather than personality attraction.

In 1997, at Transmission Gallery, Ursitti made a scent portrait of Judy Garland. *The Smell of Fear, Part One and Two: Judy Garland* reproduced the odour of the Hollywood actress who was said to have suffered from extreme body odour owing to complications arising from her drug addiction exacerbated by the stress of live performances. Ursitti replicated this scent and combined it with the perfumes that Garland was said to have used in an attempt to mask it.

In the same way that *Eau Claire* and *The Smell of Fear, Part One and Two: Judy Garland* are portraits, *Sub Club, August 8, 1998, Glasgow*, 1998, is a portrait of a night-club. The atmosphere of the club was sampled on the 8th August 1998, analysed and replicated by Dodd and Ursitti. RT

Sub Club, August 8, 1998, Glasgow 1998
synthesised scent · courtesy the artist

Alison **Watt**

Born in Greenock in 1965, Alison Watt studied in the Painting Department at Glasgow School of Art both as an undergraduate and a post-graduate. Her self-portrait won the National Portrait Gallery's competition in 1987. Watt's first solo exhibitions were in 1990 at the Scottish Gallery, London and Kelvingrove Art Gallery in Glasgow in 1991. Her 1997 exhibition, *Fold*, was shown at The Fruitmarket Gallery, Edinburgh, Aberdeen Art Gallery and Leeds Metropolitan University Gallery. Most recently an exhibition of her new work, *Shift*, was held at the Scottish National Gallery of Modern Art in Edinburgh in 2000.

From her early portrayals of the human figure and especially of the female nude, the focus of Alison Watt's more recent works has been on the fabric which surrounds the body. She focusses on fabric as surface, a membrane between the body and the outside world. Her meticulous paintings of fabric recall the delight in colour, texture and pattern apparent in the work of nineteenth century French painter, Jean Auguste Dominique Ingres, whose work is often referenced in the titles of Watt's paintings. Several of her most recent paintings are entirely devoid of direct allusion to the human figure and pattern, rendering only the tucks, folds and undulations in expanses of pure white fabric. These works, such as *Rivière*, exploit the notion of illusionistic depth in contrast with the flat reality of the painted surface. **KB**

'In their emptying of explicit figurative content and rejection of allegory and conceit, Watt's latest 'white' paintings also recall modernist abstraction: the combination of purity and sensuality found in an artist like Lucio Fontana, for example. And as with Fontana – of Yves Kein or Mark Rothko – Watt's new paintings possess a meditative or spiritual quality, their huge scale inviting the viewer's physical participation, his or her willingness to be 'enveloped'.'
Richard Calvocoressi in *Shift*

REFERENCE

Shift: New Works by Alison Watt,
Scottish National Gallery of Modern Art,
2000

Rivière 2000
oil on canvas · courtesy the artist and Aberdeen Art Gallery

Cathy **Wilkes**

Born in Belfast in 1966, Cathy Wilkes studied at Glasgow School of Art and on the MFA course at the University of Ulster, which she completed in 1992. In 1989 she was one of the founding members of Glasgow Women's Library. She had her first solo show in 1991 at Transmission Gallery, Glasgow. In 1994 she started organising exhibitions in her flat, Dalriada, in Glasgow. Since 1997 she has made collaborative work together with Victoria Morton, Sue Tompkins, Hayley Tompkins and Sarah Tripp as Elizabeth Go. In 1999 Wilkes was commissioned to produce a series of souvenirs to celebrate the opening of Dundee Contemporary Arts. In 2000 she was short listed for the inaugural Becks Futures Prize. In 2001 she had solo exhibitions at Giti Nourbakhsch, Berlin, and, *Our Misfortune* at Transmission Gallery, Glasgow. She lives and works in Glasgow and teaches at Duncan of Jordanstone College of Art and Design, Dundee.

Cathy Wilkes' work presents a formal vocabulary that describes personal experience; physical, social or political. A series of untitled rings from 1992, made in bronze and steel were the first in an on-going series of diagrammatic, still-life sculpture. These precisely crafted apertures were made as articulations of open space. Their mirrored surface is intended to reflect and absorb the light and colour of their surroundings.

Mister So and So, 2001, is one of several works made by Wilkes in recent years that utilise folding furniture. Stylised eyes, a mouth, ears and hair, all cut from printed fabrics, are placed upon a pink and white striped table top. Like Wilkes' untitled rings *Mister So and So* is intended to look back at the viewer like a mirror. *Mister So and So* is one component from a series of 'portraits', exhibited at Galerie Giti Nourbakhsch in Berlin, that includes works entitled *Psychologist* and *Mister Komplex*. **RT**

'Some artwork is intended to draw attention to the room around it, it might relate to the architecture, or the changing light, or the conditions of its making. Wilkes' work seems to draw attention to the very air in the room, and to the amazing fact of its own presence. It's like looking at 19th century photographs, with their long exposures that don't so much freeze a moment as allow it to coalesce and settle, become absorbed into the flat chemistry of the plate. Some of Daguerre's early Paris cityscapes are like that, eerily devoid of people – just to walk down the street was to move too fast for the technology to catch you – and the effect is to heighten the stillness of the inanimate world.'

Will Bradley, 'Quiet Radical' in *Untitled No.25*, Summer 2001

Mister So and So (detail) 2001
printed fabric, folding table · courtesy the artist, The Modern Institute and Galerie Giti Nourbakhsch, Berlin

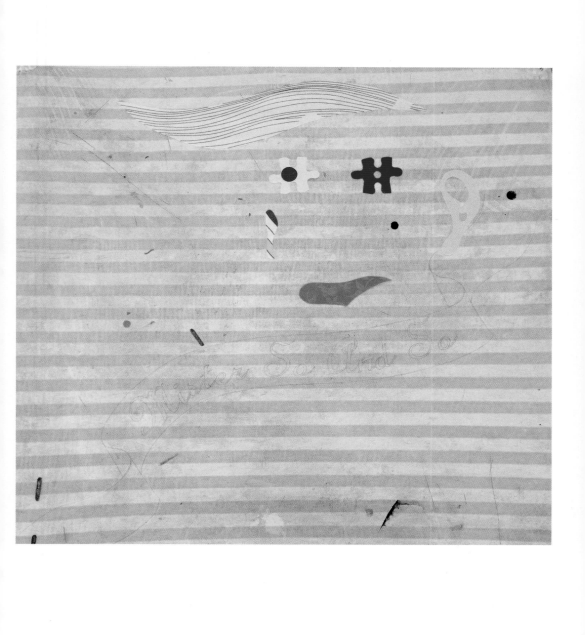

Michael **Wilkinson**

Born in Wallasey in 1965, Wilkinson studied in the Environmental Art Department at Glasgow School of Art graduating in 1998. He has had solo exhibitions at the Collective Gallery, Edinburgh and at The Modern Institute, Glasgow. Wilkinson has exhibited extensively in Scotland and participated in *Circles #4* at ZKM, Karlsruhe, 2001. 2001 also sees a major public art commission in Kiel as part of the city-wide project *Changes Possible*. Wilkinson lives and works in Glasgow.

Michael Wilkinson's work is concerned with the way in which cultural signs can be abstracted and distilled and yet still remain recognisable to wide sub cultures. Recent works have been directly informed by his interest in the music industry particularly the way in which attitudes and ideas are presented in vinyl packaging.

Coda, 2000, consists of four cardboard boxes of uniformly square paintings. These monochromatic objects; in blue, red, black and yellow, recall early Modernist painting and yet their format, 12" square, and their casual arrangement suggests that they are paintings of records. The work is intended to mix a Modern vocabulary with a car boot sale aesthetic – to reintroduce homespun creativity to a pure aesthetic. In this way the work recalls the activity of a number of electronic musicians such as Stefan Betke, Thomas Brinkman and Kit Clayton who make their music available through small, often self initiated record labels. All have championed minimal, utilitarian sleeve designs.

Record Collection, 2000, is an ongoing project to document every record in Wilkinson's expanding collection. Although pared of their original text and image, and reduced to an abstract design, each painting is instantly recognisable to those that own the same pressing. **RT**

Coda 2000
emulsion paint on board, cardboard boxes · courtesy the artist and The Modern Institute

Richard **Wright**

Born 1960 in London, Richard Wright studied painting at Edinburgh College of Art (1978–82) and later completed an MA at Glasgow School of Art (1993–95). His first solo show was at Transmission Gallery, Glasgow in 1994. He was included in *New Art in Scotland* at the CCA, Glasgow and Aberdeen Art Gallery in 1994 and *Manifesta 2* in Luxembourg. Since then Wright has participated in many international exhibitions. A solo exhibition was held at Inverleith House, Royal Botanic Garden, Edinburgh in 1999 and the following year he was included in the *British Art Show 5* and *Intelligence: New British Art* at Tate Britain. His most recent solo exhibition was at Kunsthalle Bern. He lives in Glasgow.

REFERENCE

Richard Wright, Locus +, Newcastle / Milton Keynes Gallery, 2000

Wright's paintings negotiate a space and time between the most permanent of objects – buildings – and the most ephemeral of imagery as it exists in memory. Working directly with the spaces and on the surfaces of the buildings in which he exhibits, Wright's works are short-lived, site-specific, often elaborate painted interruptions in the architecture and dynamics of the exhibition place. His imagery shifts from the resolutely modern, geometrical and abstract to the whorls of gothic ornamentation to the most prevalent and kitsch emblems of mass-produced popular culture. The kind of repertoire from which Wright draws is a world of images familiar to all from Renaissance art to MTV, all levelled in his practice by his meticulous and laborious hand-painting. While they acknowledge the history of painting and of image-making, they simultaneously insist on the physicality of our approach to the image in the gallery, taking position in very specific and intentional points in any given space.

The cycle of Wright's works is completed as, when the wall paintings are recovered with white emulsion at the end of each exhibition, they in themselves come to exist only as memories. KB

'When you enter a room housing one of his works, for a split second it seems empty. Then you might notice a small patch of coloured pattern near the floor, or running up one edge of a corner. Occasionally you won't see it until you've turned around to leave. Reminiscent of sculpture, or perhaps more accurately, modest pieces of furniture or personal belongings, they occupy the room in a completely original way.'
Alex Farquharson in *Frieze*, issue 58

Untitled work from **TeclaSala, Barcelona** 1999
gouache wall painting · courtesy the artist and The Modern Institute

Beyond the Gallery

One of the remarkable aspects of the development of art in Scotland in the years 1990–2001 has been beyond the gallery walls in 'public space'. Both commissioned projects and independent initiatives have explored the ability of art to engage in diverse contexts and situations. From permanently sited sculptural works, to short-term interventions and ephemeral projects, these works have taken art out into the wider world. **Here + Now** includes documentation of a small selection of some of the most outstanding projects to have taken place.

Claire Barclay in collaboration with architect Chris Platt

Govanhill Millennium Park
1999

Solar powered timber structure housing community resource to facilitate garden project (containing tools, greenhouse, library and observation platform), Glasgow.

Commissioned by Govanhill Housing Association

Managed by Visual Art Projects and Rock DCM

left **Paul Carter**

Signal Hut 2001

Satellite broadcasting equipment
installed within Royston Hill Spire
Royston, Glasgow.

*Commissioned by The Centre for the
Royston Road Project*

right **Nathan Coley**
Urban Sanctuary:
A Public Art Work 1997

80 page book

*Commissioned by Stills Gallery,
Edinburgh*

Managed by IPA

**Matthew Dalziel
and Louise Scullion**

Modern Nature 2001

Six solar panels mounted on five
metre high aluminium supports. The
panels power an audio recording of
the Capercallie, a bird not sighted in
the area for fifteen years. Elrick Hill,
Aberdeenshire.

*Commissioned by The Tyrebagger
Trust*

*Managed by Art in Partnership,
Edinburgh*

Jacqueline Donachie

The Trees, The Book and
The Disc 1999

Planting of seven monkey puzzle trees,
construction of a cement platform and
publication of a book documenting the
process. Darnley, Glasgow.

*Commissioned by Visual Art Projects
for the Darnley 2000 Consortium*

Anne Elliot

Tight Knit 1995

Portraits of the population of
Newcastleton, Roxburghshire
Newcastleton. [Anne Elliot: born 1962,
Carlisle, Studied Painting at Glasgow
School of Art, graduated 1985, lives
and works in Glasgow.]

*Self initiated project for Fotofeis
International Festival of Photography
1995*

Graham Fagen

Royston Road Trees 2000

Planting of 15 trees that were
dedicated to individuals by the local
community Royston, Glasgow.

*Commissioned by The Centre for the
Royston Road Project*

Douglas Gordon

Empire 1998

Neon sign fitting. Glasgow

*Commissioned by Visual Art
Projects, Glasgow for the Merchant
City Civic Society, Glasgow*

Kenny Hunter

Four Children 1998 (detail)

Bronze
Quarry Street, Hamilton

*Commissioned by South Lanarkshire
County Council*

Steven Hurrell

Zones, an Audiology of the River Clyde

13–14 November 1999

'Audio boat trip' along the River Clyde. [Stephen Hurrell: born 1965, Glasgow, studied at Glasgow School of Art, graduated 1988, lives and works in Glasgow.]

Commissioned by Tramway, Glasgow

Peter McCaughey

Arc 10–19 December 1999

Installation and film at derelict ABC Cinema, Sauchiehall Street, Glasgow. [Peter McCaughey: born 1964, Omagh, studied at York Street Art College Belfast, Glasgow School of Art and Duncan of Jordanstone College of Art and Design, completed his studies in 1988, lives and works in Glasgow.]

Commissioned by Tramway, Glasgow.

Jonathan Monk

Cancelled 1990

Fly-posted 'Cancelled' signs, Glasgow.
[Jonathan Monk: born 1969, Leicester,
Studied in the Environmental Art
Department of Glasgow School of Art,
graduated 1991, lives and works in
Berlin.]

Self initiated project

Donald Urquhart

Birked Scar 1999

Fifteen metre square burnt into heather
and marked by 200 silver birch trees,
Elrick Hill, Aberdeenshire.

Commissioned by the Tyrebagger Trust

Managed by Art in Partnership, Edinburgh

Scottish Art since 1945

A series of four exhibitions over four years organised as a collaboration between Aberdeen Art Gallery, Dundee Contemporary Arts and McManus Galleries, Dundee.

Into the New Age
1945–1962

Aberdeen Art Gallery
29 August - 17 October 1998
McManus Galleries, Dundee
31 October 1998 – 9 January 1999

Donald Bain, Wilhemina Barns-Graham, James Cowie, Robert Colquhoun, William Crosbie, Hugh Adam Crawford, Alan Davie, Joan Eardley, J. D. Fergusson, Ian Fleming, Alan Fletcher, William Gear, Stephen Gilbert, William Gillies, George Innes, William Johnstone, Jack Knox, Hew Lorimer, Robert MacBryde, William McCance, William MacTaggart, Oscar Marzaroli, John Maxwell, Alberto Morrocco, Lil Neilson, J McIntosh Patrick, Eduardo Paolozzi, Robin Philipson, Anne Redpath, Benno Schotz, William Turnbull, William Wilson
Selected by Iain Gale
Sponsored by Robert Fleming Holdings Limited

Liberation & Tradition
1963–1975

Aberdeen Art Gallery
5 June – 31 July 1999
McManus Galleries, Dundee
14 August – 17 October 1999

Wilhelmina Barns-Graham, John Bellany, Elizabeth Blackadder, Mark Boyle, William Burns, Fred Bushe, Vincent Butler, John Byrne, Robert Callender, Peter Collins, Alan Davie, Ken Dingwall, David Donaldson, Patricia Douthwaite, Ian Hamilton Finlay, John Houston, James Howie, William Johnstone, Jack Knox, Gerald Laing, David McClure, Ian McCulloch, Joseph McKenzie, Will Maclean, Bruce McLean, Ian McLeod, Alexander Moffat, James Morrison, Alberto Morrocco, Eduardo Paolozzi, Robin Philipson, Barbara Rae, Gavin Scobie, Ian McKenzie Smith, Ainslie Yule
Selected by Victoria Keller
Sponsored by Aberdeen Asset Management

Expressions
1976–1989

Aberdeen Art Gallery
10 June – 22 July 2000
Dundee Contemporary Arts and McManus Galleries, Dundee
16 September – 5 November 2000

Sam Ainslie, John Bellany, Elizabeth Blackadder, Fred Bushe, Joyce Cairns, Robert Callender, Steven Campbell, Fionna Carlisle, Martin Churchill, Doug Cocker, Calum Colvin, Stephen Conroy, David Cook, Thomas Joshua Cooper, Ken Currie, Alexander Fraser, Ian Hamilton Finlay, Ronald Forbes, Lys Hansen, Gwen Hardie, Jake Harvey, Ian Howard, Peter Howson, Ian Hughes, Callum Innes, Ian Johnston, Murray Johnston, Jake Kempsell, Eileen Lawrence, Owen Logan, David Mach, Ian McCulloch, Patricia Macdonald, Robert Maclaurin, John McLean, Will Maclean, Bruce McLean, Caroline McNairn, Pradip Malde, Alexander Moffat, Ron O'Donnell, Elizabeth Ogilvie, Glen Onwin, Roger Palmer, Jacki Parry, Barbara Rae, June Redfern, Alan Robb, Colin Ruscoe, Gavin Scobie, Bill Scott, Ian McKenzie Smith, Ruth Stirling, Linda Taylor, William Turnbull, Alan Watson, Arthur Watson, Alison Watt, Kate Whiteford, David Williams, Adrian Wiszniewski
Selected by Victoria Keller
Sponsored by Aberdeen Asset Management

Acknowledgements

For their assistance and support in producing the exhibition and this publication, we would like to extend our thanks to: Ami Barak; Susanna Beaumont; Jörn Bötnagel; Lucy Byatt; Cabinet Gallery, London; John Calcutt; The Centre, Glasgow; Sadie Coles; Laurent Delaye; Alan Dimmick (photographs pages 17-24); doggerfisher, Edinburgh; Judith Findlay; Stephen Friedman Gallery, London; Johnny Hanna; Richard Ingleby; Iain Irving; Maria Lind; Euan McArthur; Martin McGeown; Andrew Mummery; Andrew Nairne; Newland Electronics Ltd.; Anthony Reynolds Gallery, London; Lisson Gallery, London; The Modern Institute, Glasgow; Visual Art Projects, Glasgow; Toby Webster; Andrew Weatley; Angela Weight.

In Aberdeen: Deirdre Grant, Jennifer Melville and David Atherton at Aberdeen Art Gallery; Lindsay Gordon, Colin Greenslade and Susan Grant at Peacock Visual Arts.

In Dundee: Fiona Bond, Sarah Derrick, Colin Lindsay, Jeni Iannetta, Miriam Lea, Jane O'Neill at Dundee Contemporary Arts; Norrie Colston, Elaine Milne, Janice Murray and Joe Sage at Dundee City Council Arts & Heritage (McManus Galleries); Mary Anderson, John Carroll, Jill Herbert, Derrick Lodge; John Louden, Tony Nolan and Aileen Stackhouse at Generator Projects; and Gary Thomson at Jute café-bar.

Lenders to the exhibition

The artists and several private collections
Aberdeen Art Gallery and Museums
British Council, London
FRAC Languedoc-Roussillon, Montpellier
Leeds Museums and Art Galleries
Imperial War Museum, London
Migros Museum, Zürich
Neugerriemschneider, Berlin
Scottish National Gallery of Modern Art
National Museum and Galleries on Merseyside
(Walker Art Gallery, Liverpool)

**Books are to be returned on or before
the last date below.**

7 – DAY
LOAN